PERSPECTIVES

MY LIFE, TIMES & CONVICTIONS

CHAPTER I 2
THE BOOMER YEARS 1947 - 1965

CHAPTER II 29
THE PRODUCTIVE YEARS 1947 - 1965

CHAPTER III 55
RELIGION & SPIRITUALITY RECONSIDERED

CHAPTER IV 80
WHAT I LEARNED ABOUT LEADERSHIP

CHAPTER V 105
TITANS OF PERFORMANCE

CHAPTER VI 130
ACHIEVING CORPORATE COMPLIANCE EXCELLENCE

CHAPTER VII 155
FIFTY SHADES OF TRUMP

PERSPECTIVES

MY LIFE, TIMES & CONVICTIONS

CHAPTER I

MY LIFE & TIMES
THE "BOOMER YEARS" 1947 - 1965

CONTENTS

Dedication	3
Preface	3
Hometown	4
Home Sweet Home	5
Mom & Dad	6
Romance	10
Family	10
Toddlers	12
Boyhood	12
School K-8	13
Playmates	15
Church	16
Sports	17
Sundays	19
The Lakes	19
Christmas	20
Silver Beach	21
Easter	22
Halloween	22
High School	22
Tiger Teams	23
Social Life	24
The Future	25

DEDICATED TO MY WONDERFUL WIFE ANGELINE

PREFACE

I am a member of the large post-war "Baby Boomers" generation, 1946 – 1964, the span of years covered in this autobiography. To highlight life back then, technologies we take for granted now were nowhere to be seen in those years:

- When I was a hospital CEO in 1980, I had installed the hospital's first computer, a small IBM mainframe installed in the business department. We were still using the IBM Selectric typewriters.

- My medical staff at that time were tethered to land-line phones so they could respond immediately for emergencies when 'on call.' The world's first cell phone was launched in 1983. It was the Motorola DynaTAC 800x. It was priced at around $4,000 and lasted for 30 minutes of talk time before dying.

- Full commercial deployment of the Internet in the U.S. did not occur until in 1995. The *World Wide Web* was the thing of science fiction back then.

For baby boomers, this twenty-year period was a time of growing prosperity for the U.S. middle class and families dined together without the distractions of cell phones and tablets.

HOMETOWN

The Nusbaum family resided in the suburb of Lakeview, adjacent to Battle Creek (hereafter, "B.C."), Michigan, a city of about 45,000 in the early 1950's. B.C. was settled around 1831. Legend has it the name was coined after a minor skirmish in March 1824, between a federal government land survey party led by Colonel John Mullett and two Potawatomi Indians. One surveyor shot and seriously wounding one of the Indians.

B.C. was the home of abolitionist Sojourner Truth (1797 – 1883) after her escape from slavery. The city was a major stop on the *Underground Railroad* used by fugitive slaves to reach freedom in Michigan. After her death in B.C. in November 1883, Frederick Douglass offered a eulogy for her: *"Venerable for age, distinguished for insight into human nature, remarkable for independence and courageous self-assertion, devoted to the welfare of her race, she has been for the last forty years an object of respect and admiration to social reformers everywhere."*

The Seventh-day Adventist Church figured prominently in B.C.'s history. Two congregation members, John Harvey, and William Kieth (W.K.) Kellogg, operated the Battle Creek Sanitarium health resort and invented cereal flakes that made the name Kellogg's famous. B.C. is now known as the *'Cereal Capital'* of the world. C.W. Post, a patient at the Sanitarium, also became a cereal entrepreneur and made *Post* cereals another extremely popular brand. Today, Kellogg's remains the dominant industry in B.C.

HOME SWEET HOME

Our home on 22nd Street was a typical middle-class neighborhood of modest bungalows. Dad bought this home new and finished-off the upstairs into two dormer bedrooms of knotty pine paneling. Twin brother, Joel and I had shared one dormer room and sister, Kay, in the other. I suspect this location was chosen due to its proximity to the Catholic church and elementary school on the next street. These neighborhoods would be at the center of my universe during my 'boomer years'.

MOM & DAD

Jennie (Lewandowski) Nusbaum was born on September 16, 1919, in Dowagiac, Michigan, about 60 miles southwest of B.C. One of six girls and one boy, Jennie was in the middle of the sibling lineup: Sabina, Stella, Anna, Jennie, Henry, Mary, and Helen. Her parents, Ignace, and Mary, immigrated from Poland. After landing at Ellis Island, they each settled in Chicago. By 1900, 23 Polish Catholic parishes were located throughout Chicago. For non-English speakers, the parish community was undoubtedly a great comfort and anchor when trying to establish a new life in a new land. There, Ignace, and Mary met and wed, and later finally relocated in Dowagiac, on the other side of Lake Michigan.

Ignace was an upper middle-class, well-educated Pole. He left Poland after being confronted with mandatory conscription into the Russian army which he absolutely refused to do. Mary (Krazinski) Lewandowski was a diminutive lady who was submissive to her domineering husband. Dowagiac, about eighty miles east of Chicago, had a population of around 5,000 residents. Nevertheless, there was a large enough Polish community and active Catholic parish life to make them feel at home. The motivation was undoubtedly employment. Ignace went to work for the Round Oak Stove Co., a firm synonymous with heating stoves in the late 1800s and the major Dowagiac industry. My grandparents never spoke English fluently and I do not believe they ever drove an auto. When we visited once or twice a year, there was no communication beyond greetings, smiles and hugs.

Mom said she was somewhat the favorite daughter; her dad picked her to walk him to work nearby carrying his lunch bucket. The factory was a polluted smoke-heavy foundry. Years later, Ignace suffered from silicosis, a pulmonary fibrosis lung disease caused by breathing bits of silica.

I often asked Mom to recount and repeat stories from her childhood. Three reminisces stood out in particular: one tragic, one depressing and another sad yet somewhat humorous.

1. Mom's only brother, Henry, was about age 8 when he drowned in a large pond near their home. Years later, when I worked at the Dowagiac's Lee Memorial Hospital, I drove past that body of water daily. It was about a mile down Division Street from their family home. During wintertime, Henry and his playmates must have figured the pond was safely iced over. Somehow, Henry fell through and could not find the surface or get rescued. In those days, bodies were laid out in the home before burial. This must have been terribly traumatic for the family, their relatives, and friends. Jennie

recalled being mortified when, soon after the burial, her dad took her to the barber shop insisting she get a *page-style* haircut. Jennie was the only daughter with jet black hair like Henry's; the other girls were strawberry blonds. Jennie's new *pageboy* helped keep Henry's memory alive for the desperately grieving family. It was humiliation for Jennie.

2. The Lewandowski's struggled like most families during the *Great Depression* from 1929 onward. They survived by picking berries. SW Michigan is wine country and conducive to growing grapes and other fruits. Mom recalled putting on a broad brimmed hat and arm coverings to protect from the sun. The family was driven by truck to berry patches where Jennie's job was to carry the berries picked by the family to a shed where she was given tokens for each container. At day's end, the tokens were exchanged for cash. That is how they managed through those difficult years.

3. Mom said her parents were extremely frugal and knew how to use a butchered pig from snout to tail. This included smoking parts as they had a small smokehouse in the backyard. When a little girl, she must have done something stupid and caused a fire that destroyed that smokehouse. Scared, she recalls running from her father bent on giving her a thrashing.

Despite these periods of trauma, mom spoke mostly of a happy childhood. Her church youth group activities, Saturday night polka dances at the parish hall, and spending summers at a nearby lake with her favorite aunt and cousin were among her fondest memories. A mature, confident, and selfless woman, Jennie left for Battle Creek to work and discover her destiny.

John William Nusbaum Sr. was the center of attention in our home, larger than life. He 'ruled the roost'. Mom was the dutiful, submissive homemaker that was typical of the time. Dad was compassionate, not a dominating man, but he needed to be the center of attraction. Deeply insecure with a needy self-centeredness, Dad claimed this was partly due to his mom dropping him off in a park all day, alone and unsupervised, at a tender age during the Depression while she sold mutual funds door to door trying to keep the family afloat.

Dad did not mention his parent's background so my knowledge of his father, John R., who died in 1948 shortly after my birth, is paltry. I was told he had a keen sense of humor, and it seems that his wife, Alice, was more ambitious and the main breadwinner while raising four children. She enjoyed longevity, living just two years shy of one hundred years.

Dad's surname "Nusbaum" is German for *Nus* -'nut' and *Baum* -'tree'" and his mother's maiden name, "Wilson" is English. Beyond that, I know nothing of Dad's heritage.

Born two years after Mom, in 1921, in Kankakee, Illinois, John -- who was called *Jack* all his life -- was a highly capable man. Intelligent, handsome, personable, a gifted writer and a respected Marine and corporate executive. Following his tenure in the U.S. Marines where he served in the South Pacific as a Chief Warrant Officer, he returned to become a supervisor at a large B.C. steel & wire company. Through talent and ambition, he rose to become its Vice President and served in that capacity until his retirement.

Tragedy struck the Nusbaum's home just as it did the Lewandowski's. Oldest son, Henry, about age 11, died from an accidental hanging in his bedroom. We were told he was playing with his belt and somehow slipped horsing around. This somber event had to traumatize Jack, the second oldest, and his sister Rosanna and youngest boy, our Uncle Gene.

ROMANCE

Jennie moved to B.C. to take a clerical position at Eaton Corporation and needed a place to live. A co-worker and soon to become her best friend, Rosanna Nusbaum, invited her to rent a room in their house. This was the eventful decision that would spark a romance when Dad returned for a short leave from the service. In his snappy Marine Corps dress uniform, Jennie was smitten from the start and Jack reciprocated. Mom's favorite songs was *"Smoke Gets in Your Eyes"*. As far as Jack was concerned, that smoke never cleared.

Jack did not waste time and was not the kind of guy to deny himself anything. The romance turned quickly to courtship sped along by Dad's duty to return to active service in the Marine Corps. I imagine the 'charm offensive' was intense and irresistible for Mom. The proposal was made and accepted without hesitation.

Time of the essence, Jack & Jennie wed in Dowagiac's Holy Maternity of Mary Church and then drove a mere thirteen miles southwest to honeymoon at *Four Flags Hotel* in Niles, MI., just north of South Bend, IN. With his bride by his side, Jack returned to active duty no doubt with a wide grin on his face and eagerness to start a family with Jennie after the war ended. That opportunity came quickly.

FAMILY

While stationed at Camp Lejeune living in a Quonset hut, the Nusbaum couple became a family on Friday, August 11, 1945, with the arrival of Karen Kay ("KK" or "Kay") just three days before President Harry Truman announced that Japan had surrendered unconditionally. Kay would be the only girl to grace the family. It must have had quite a celebration: a new baby girl and a world finally at peace.

With the war effort winding down, Jack was given an honorable discharge and the young family moved back to Battle Creek. Dad found work at United Steel & Wire Co., a manufacturer of grocery carts. Its largest customer was the A&P grocery chain. He began as a supervisor and ended his career there as its Vice President through diligence and leadership qualities.

Not long after their return to B.C., Jennie was again in the 'family way'. While both were excited no doubt, Jennie also was anxious. Her very painful first delivery made her forever dread giving birth. Her dread must have multiplied exponentially when they learned twins were expected. Dad, not burdened with pregnancy, was so 'pumped-up', he promised Mom a new fur coat if the twins were boys. He paid up. On Friday, September 5, 1947, yours truly and brother Joel took their first breaths. Mom's belly nearly bursting, she delivered premature fraternal twin, each under five pounds. It was 'touch-n-go' in the beginning. Joel, they said, was in a crisis. We were placed in incubators with high concentrations of oxygen that severely damaged our eyes; a complication not understood by medical science at that time. It was the price for staying alive.

In 1953, the Nusbaum clan greeted its fourth sibling, Charles (Chuck) Kent. It would be another six years before Gregory (Greg) Lee joined to complete our clan.

TODDLERS

We both managed to survive. I was born six minutes ahead of Joel, but Joel claims he was conceived first, so I could not gloat much. Out of danger, the doctor told Mom she could take better care of us at home, and so she did. She said each of us could fit inside a shoe box when we came home. Surviving turned into thriving thanks to Mom's constant attention and Dad's help when home. Having three in diapers was a huge challenge. Mom was grateful she had a washing machine and dryer.

Mom said when she changed our diapers, my hands were open and relaxed; Joel held his hands into tight fists. These were clues that we quite different personalities from the start.

BOYHOOD

As fraternal twins, you might suspect we would not look alike, but we managed to fool quite of few people especially when Mom dressed us alike. My eyes were more crossed than Joel's, so I was a candidate for strabismus surgery on both eyes at age 5. My only recollection is of Mom reading to me with my eye patches on. *Peter Pan* was one of them. Although this correction helped a great deal, I never had 20/20 vision nor good depth perception, so had difficulty reading, hitting curve balls, and shooting basketballs. Since the rest of the family had perfect vision, I credit that oxygen filled incubator for these vision troubles. But that did not stop Joel and me from having a fabulous boyhood.

Dad was raised a Methodist. At Mom's urging, he agreed to convert to Catholicism, and he became an active and devoted member of our parish. This was the main cause of tension between my Dad's mother and Mom. When Grandma suggested Mom let the children choose between Methodism and Catholicism when they were older, Mom 'hit the roof'.

I will describe my boyhood in five general themes: School, Playmates, Church, Sports and Special Occasions. Most of these Joel and I experienced together. These were the reoccurring themes and rhythms of our lives that took us through our first eighteen years until 1965 we left home for college in the Fall. Thereafter, we only returned for summer jobs or to visit.

SCHOOL K-8

My earliest recollections get a bit better about the time we went to kindergarten. We attended Prairieview Kindergarten for half days in the afternoons. It was about one-half mile from home, so Mom took each of our hands and walked us there and returned for us each day. We each had one graham cracker and small bottle of milk for our snack break. I remember that best. We had our little rug to unroll when it was time for naps. So, I remember the food and the nap, not much else. Oh, we had one or two ice-cream socials. I suppose my fondest memories come from my stomach. We were both very shy kids; I do not recall socializing at that stage.

The next eight years we attended St. Joseph elementary next to our parish church of the same name. The Sisters of St. Joseph nuns along with lay teachers taught us. My favorite teacher was Sr. Fidelis, a young sister I had for first grade. I recall learning to read and spell with a box of alphabets. Sister had us put letters onto our desks to form and recite words. A couple of years later, I auditioned with her for the boys' choir. I still remember the song she had me sing, *"Sweetly sings the donkey as he goes to hay, someone must go with him or he'll run away, kiai kio kiai kio kiay …. And repeat."* I only song I can remember to this day. I had a mediocre voice, but somehow made the cut and joined the boys' choir. This was not the Vienna Boys Choir.

Perhaps because of my poor eyesight, I had difficulty reading yet seemed to be able to finish in the middle of my class rankings usually with a B or B+ average. Joel was usually ahead of me academically; he was the always the more studious twin.

PLAYMATES

Joel and I got along well. We rarely quarreled. He was my constant playmate and friend. I was the dominant twin, but Joel held his own. I was more gregarious and sociable; Joel was more introverted, reflective and to himself. We both were shy with strangers. Yet, at home, we were typical outgoing, rambunctious boys. We had bunk beds with a ladder in our upstairs room. Sometimes, Dad separated them into side-by-side beds. Before sleeping, we usually played word games like, "My father owns a grocery store; he sells something that begins with B". The guessing started and then it was the other guy's turn. That was our nighttime ritual. I would never know what an only child felt like and was glad to have a constant companion.

Our neighborhood had a large gully at the end of our street. It sloped steeply forming a hillside. In the winter, we took our sleds there and had great fun. In the summer, we played war there.

There were also wild blackberry patches. We would go picking and filling quart containers. Selling these and Cub Scout cookies door to door were our first attempts at entrepreneurship.

Mark was the boyfriend we shared. He lived on the next street, and we were constant companions. My most vivid memories of Mark were playing with marbles. It was not the normal game of marbles on the ground in a circle. We had our own version. Standing, the first player tossed his marble a few feet away. The other guy tossed his as close as he could to the other. As these marbles got nearer to each other, a player would pick up his marble, hold it belt high and, like a bombardier, try to drop it and hit the other fellow's marble. If successful, that player picked up both and kept them. If not, the other guy tried and took turns until someone hit the target. After hours, someone left home with a much larger cache of cat's eye marbles.

I had one boyfriend with whom I remained in contact my entire life. John was a unique person. A bit obnoxious which I could tolerate easily while others could not, I admired his strong points. John was very bright and a great friend. He shared interests with me. He was a rock collector, interested in astronomy and liked science fiction. His mom made the best sloppy Joe's. And unlike myself, John always seemed to have cash on hand. And he was always generous with his money. We would often walk and talk our way to the diary store a mile away and he treated me to countless ice cream cones. John went to law school in New York City and still practices real estate law in the Yonkers, New York area until today.

CHURCH

Mom's Catholic devotion and parochial school steeped us in religion. Around fourth grade we wanted to become altar servers. The Mass was completely in Latin then. To qualify, we had to memorize Latin verses beginning with *"Ad Deum qui laetificat juventutem meam"*. Also, the "Confiteor" and *"Suscipiat"*. Joel and I mastered the Latin, passed our auditions and were proud to be altar servers. We became favorites because we looked like matched candle sticks. We were always picked when the bishop came to the parish. Our heroes were parish priests from then on. One day when I was 10 or 11, I was walking with our parish pastor on the school playground while he was giving his Irish Setter a run. He asked me what I wanted to do when I grew up. I said I wanted to become the Pope. This tickled him for sure. But I was dead serious.

In our basement, Joel and I set up an altar and we constantly played saying Mass down there. We perfected all the moves the priest routinely does at the altar. We had our own chalice and filled it with *Necco* candy wafers for practicing giving out communion. We imagined becoming priests from these formative years onward and this desire hardened and remained strong culminating in our entry into a seminary after high school. The sisters' convent was a block away. There was 8 – 10 nuns and they had a little chapel in their convent. On Saturdays, the parish priest said Mass there. He would call me to come serve as the altar server. So, I would ride my bicycle over to the convent to assist the priest. The sisters often asked our family to go to the bakery for them. Their favorite was hot cross buns.

SPORTS

Dad was an avid sports fan and it rubbed off. Our back yard was our sports park. We played football in the fall. We played catch in the summer. In winter, Dad even flooded the back yard, so we had an ice rink to play hockey. When we were not playing, we were watching on TV. Dad was a die-hard *Detroit Tiger, Lion* and *Red Wings* fan. Mom complained that on weekends Dad had a TV and radio on and you dare not disturb him. Each team had its superstars and we cheered them on.

Our biggest thrill was when Dad took us to Detroit to Briggs Stadium to watch the Tigers. Nothing better than hot dogs, peanuts, and a win. If we were not in the back yard or watching on TV, we were at the school ball diamond in the summer or in the lot next to the school to play football in the fall with our boyfriends. Summers meant constant trips to the ball diamond.

We entered organized baseball early. I was slow and tall for my age, so I became a catcher. My first team was the St. Joe Orioles around the fourth grade and my catching skills got better and better as the years rolled forward. I was always on some team every summer, Joel to a lesser extent but also highly active in baseball. Dad coached teams we joined. When Joel and I walked home from the ballpark on Columbia Rd., we always dropped into McDonalds to get a bag of delicious French fries. In those days, the potatoes were not frozen. Huge bags of spuds and a potato peeler in plain view in the back of the store.

SUNDAYS

Sundays were special. After Mass, Dad helped serve coffee and donuts in the parish basement. Mom cooked a delicious dinner, usually a pot roast with mashed potatoes. After a ballgame or two, we would drive around Battle Creek for an hour or more. Mom got a break outside the home, and we loved to 'window shop' through neighborhoods admiring the pricier homes as if we would someday "move-up" into the next tier of status and luxury. It never happened, but we never tired of this ritual which always ended in a delight. Dad took us to our favorite ice cream dairy store, Sullivans. We could order whatever we wanted: double-dip ice cream cone, a chocolate malt or -- Mom's favorite -- a hot fudge sundae. That treat was the Nusbaum's way of celebrating the beginning of a new week.

THE LAKES

B.C. had a 352-acre lake within the city limits. Named after a Potawatomi tribal word 'Coquagiack', Goguac Lake and its public Willard Beach was our beach playground in the sizzling summer months. We were always thrilled when allowed to go swim at Goguac.

When Dad had vacation time, we spent weeks at Michigan lake up north renting a cottage. Dad loved to fish. We would row our boat out with our bamboo poles, box of worms and Dad's tackle box. If lucky, that evening we had pan-fried fresh blue gills or lake perch so delicious after fishing and swimming all day.

CHRISTMAS

If there one annual event that the Nusbaum clan was never outdone, it was Christmas. Dad went 'whole-hog'. He was as excited watching us rip packages open as we were doing so. Dad took us to a Christmas tree farm and picked out a nice one. Mom and Kay did most of the decorating. The excitement grew as we listened to Christmas music and the Michigan magical winter provided the festive snowfalls we loved so much.

Dad insisted Christmas gift giving be in the A.M. and not on Christmas Eve, so it was torture trying to sleep. I recall crying many times frustrated I just could not sleep, wanting morning to arrive instantly. There was method to his strictness. He hid presents in his trunk and anywhere he could hide them. We still believed in Santa, so Dad needed those wee hours to place what seemed like a treasure trove of presents under the tree.

We were gaga-eyed when we came downstairs and saw the incredible colorful displays of various sized packages overflowing under the tree and far beyond. Someone was picked to be Santa to parcel out the gifts, so everyone had their turn opening, wowing, and showing off their treasures. This was not a mere two or three gifts each. Dad lavished present after present. It took an hour or more to finish, leaving huge bags of crumple wrapping paper. Mom could not believe it but let Dad do his thing. No question, Christmas was a thrilling time to be a Nusbaum.

SILVER BEACH

Another family outing that excited us was a trek to Benton Harbor on the shore of Lake Michigan, home of *Silver Beach*, a popular amusement park. We packed a picnic lunch and headed west on I-94 for seventy-three miles. My favorite amusement rides were the tilt-a-whirl and electric bumper cars. The roller coaster was just too scary. My absolute favorite place was in the Penny Arcade. Dad gave each of a roll of coins that we had to nurse until exhausted. Carefully, I plotted each move and executed my gameplan until every dime was spent, never for a moment thinking of saving any coins or buying a treat. Those games and odd machines were just too addictive. I savored each moment.

Mom was an excellent cook. Yet, the odor I recall best outside the kitchen was when Dad opened a huge round tin can of New Era potato chips at the amusement park. The whiff hit me like a brick. Every time I open a bag of Lay's since then, I take a whiff hoping to recapture that delightful fresh potato chip fragrance.

EASTER

Aside from our dutiful religious observances for Easter season that included meatless Fridays, putting a palm branch on the wall, and getting decked-out for Easter Sunday Mass, the big event came through the post office. *Babcha*, grandma, had a specialty not passed down to her daughters: Polish Kieska. When that large post arrived filled with rings of blood sausage, we jumped for joy. Mom cut-up and browned bacon, then sauteed the kieska. My, my, we were in heaven. And if lucky, *Babcha* sent another batch at Christmastime. Mom would say in Polish, 'daj buzi' (pronounced 'day-boozhie') meaning 'give me a kiss.' I could kiss *Babcha* after each bite had she been around.

HALLOWEEN

Halloween was always a big event because it meant treats and more treats. In those days, neighborhoods were safe and as we grew older, our radius expanded. The loot became so large in later years, we carried pillowcases to collect from house to house. Escorted by Mom or Dad at first, we later ventured out alone and this sugar pilgrimage was serious stuff. After canvassing our turf and deciding enough was enough, the fun began back home sorting, discovering, counting, trading, and sampling the goodies.

The sugar high lasted a week or more when, saving the best for last, we devoured those big candy bars like *Three Musketeers*.

HIGH SCHOOL

The innocence of those childhood days ended after we graduated from St. Joseph's elementary and as we looked ahead to freshman year at St. Philip's High. The leisurely walk to school now became a bus or car ride into downtown Battle Creek each day. New and many familiar classmates joined us in our tiny class of about one hundred. Joel and I were the tallest at six feet - two inches. A different order of nuns greeted us: the 'IHMs', Servants of the Immaculate Heart of Mary. A bit sterner maybe because managing students in those teen years required more muscle.

My string of getting average grades endured during high school. I graduated with a B+ average in the middle of my class. Joel ranked higher which I admired. Not so good at math, I was more interested in and did better in literature, civics and of course religion. Looking ahead to the priesthood, I knew Latin would be stressed, so I took four years of high school Latin. Little did I know that within a scant five years after my high school graduation, the Latin Mass ended in favor of English, our vernacular. Four years of high school and twenty college credits of Latin never used except it became my minor subject for my bachelor's degree.

TIGER TEAMS

I continued to be consumed with sports during high school playing on St. Philip Tiger teams. Dad was my biggest fan. He always had an interest in photography with the best cameras and his own dark room in the basement to develop negatives. With his telephoto lens, he took shots during our sporting events. His best photos he gladly donated to the high school, and they ended up prominent in our yearbook sports section.

I excelled in football and baseball. I won the 'first-string' center position in my sophomore year in football; and, in the springtime, I became the starting baseball catcher in baseball for all four years. Even with poor eyesight, I managed to hit for a 350 average and batted 'clean-up' -- fourth -- on the rotation. But curve balls were getting tougher to see; my baseball career would end there. In senior year, my coach asked me if I wanted him to promote a sports scholarship for me. I politely declined saying my future was in a seminary. During those years, wearing my bright red varsity sweater with that large white 'P' for St. Philips on the breast was my pride and joy.

SOCIAL LIFE

Carrying a firm intent to become a priest on my sleeve, this meant a life of celibacy. While all the other guys were trying to 'sow wild oats', I simply studied, played sports and hung out with my guy friends. Still rather shy around girls anyway, and completely naïve, my relationship with girls were friendly yet aloof. I still had crushes from time to time, but they were passing fantasies and never serious. Thoughts never turned into actions. I was quite popular with the girls simply because I excelled in sports. Pursuing an exclusive girlfriend relationship never occurred to me.

Consequently, I never dated during high school with the ironic exception I took the Homecoming queen to the dance after she asked me to escort her. Molly was dating a guy who had already graduated. She wanted to go with a classmate, so knowing I was 'safe' and unattached, she approached me. I agreed. That was the extent of my coed socializing outside of the classroom with one awkward exception.

Mom said knowing how to dance was an essential life skill for a guy, whether a future priest or not. We tried to convince her otherwise, but her insistence won out. She found a neighbor lady who was teaching dance in her home and enrolled us. We grudgingly went and learned the Box-step, Watusi, Twist and other popular dances of the period. Being athletic did not seem to help. I just tolerated it.

St. Philip's had one social outlet that we flocked to during lunchtime and after school. Directly across the street, they had acquired an old factory building and remodeled the first floor into a recreation and dance hall of sorts. Called "Tiger Room" after our team mascot, this was the place to be seen and to socialize. As was typical, the guys stayed on one side and gals the other side. Guys would ask girls to dance to popular songs of the day. I just spent time together with the boys, but I remember two favorite pop songs: "Go Away Little Girl" sung by Steve Lawrence and "Hey Paula" sung by Ray Hildebrand and Jill Jackson. I departed the high school social scene totally AWOL in terms of boy-girl matters.

THE FUTURE

My 'Boomer' years were filled with love, joy, and happiness. We lived on a safe, secure cozy street with a loving family; a cocoon where a young boy could enjoy his childhood of play and imagination. Mom and Dad were affectionate, devoted parents and responsible. We lacked for nothing, were well fed, yet lived modestly. I recall having an bad case of homesickness after leaving home for the first time to enter college. But life went on.

I entered Saint Gregory Seminary with brother Joel with my priestly dreams intact. The *Civil Rights Movement* of the 1960s, the *Second Vatican Council* that began in October 1962 and President Lyndon B. Johnson's order in August 1964 that deployed combat units into the *Vietnam War* for the first time would usher a completely new religious and political landscape no one could foresee.

When General Douglas MacArthur gave his retirement speech to Congress on April 15, 1951, he said entering the Army was *"the fulfillment of my boyish hopes and dreams."* He spent 52 years living out his dreams. For me and many like me, those dreams would be dashed in the turbulent years that lie ahead.

PERSPECTIVES

MY LIFE, TIMES & PERSPECTIVES

CHAPTER II

MY LIFE & TIMES

THE PRODUCTIVE YEARS 1965 - 2008

CONTENTS

Dedication 29
Preface... 29
Saint Gregory Seminary... 29
Sacred Heart Seminary 33
Difficult Decision.. 34
Western Michigan University.................................. 34
Night House Orderly... 36
Vietnam War... 37
Wisconsin Teacher Corps... 38
Battle Creek Sanitarium...40
Borgess Hospital... 41
Nurse Staffing Coordinator..................................... 42
Unit Manager.. 42
Director of Trauma and Ambulatory Care............ 43
Lee Memorial Hospital... 45
SSJ Health System.. 47
Ascension Health.. 50

DEDICATED TO MY LOVELY DAUGHTERS

JENNIE   MARGIE   NAHKA

PREFACE

The next chapters of my life began in the Fall of 1965. In my formative years, I wrote a life script that seemed indelible from my earliest recollections. My heroes where Catholic priests. I imbibed my Polish Catholic mom's devotion reinforced during twelve years of parochial education. Even before puberty, I was committed to a single life of celibacy; it never dawned on me to date during high school. With four years of high school Latin, I was primed for the seminary. What seemed to be predestined turned into an odyssey of self-discovery.

SAINT GREGORY SEMINARY

Inquiring as early as eighth grade about entering the seminary, my parish priest counseled me to wait until after high school. Finally, that time had come. Our Lansing Diocese had no seminary, so they secured placements for me, brother Joel and several high school classmates at Saint Gregory Seminary in Cincinnati, Ohio.

Two routes are available to the Catholic priesthood. One is through in a dioecian seminary, the spawning ground for parish priests under the direction of a local bishop. The other is through a religious congregation such as the Jesuits. We chose the diocesan route. The Archdiocese of Cincinnati accepted us for entry into their minor seminary at Saint Gregory. This was an accredited college offering two majors: Philosophy and English.

We were instructed to get dental check-ups and have our clothes tagged with a certain three-digit number so the seminary laundry could keep track of our clothing. Dad and Mom escorted us on the long drive of 255 miles to Cincinnati and we bid farewell and entered our new home on Beechmont Avenue.

Saint Gregory was among the most regimented diocesan seminaries in the U.S. It ran more like a bootcamp than a college campus. Rules included "Grand Silence" meaning no talking after evening prayers until after breakfast grace was recited by the Rector, the seminary director. That meant no communication with your roommates in the evenings. It was prohibited to entry any other students' rooms. Wake-up at 5:55 A.M. sharp and we had about 20 minutes to get to the chapel. If late getting to your assigned seat, you had to kneel during the entire service in the isle. Each day was completely structured into chapel services, meals, classes, recreation time and study time.

Because I had four years of high school Latin, I began a typical Freshman year. However, Joel and my other classmates who took fewer years of high school Latin were put into remedial Latin classes; and their freshman courses were delayed one full year.

I had a severe case of homesickness but weathered through it. Having Joel near was an immense help. The campus was beautiful. We had wonderful professors like Rev. George Berwanger, our English literature professor. And of course, we made friends. So gradually, I was able to adjust to the regimen away from home.

Another draconian rule was no opportunity to leave the campus until holiday or summer vacation. This felt like a cloister. There were no girls on campus, save for few kitchen helpers. Mainly, nuns took care of the chores with our assistance. Whenever we were about to leave the campus, the sermons were always a warning to beware of girls.

To demonstrate the strictness observed, Beechmont Avenue sloped upward in front of the grounds. One winter day, there was an icy mixture causing cars to barely make it up that grade. Seeing this and wanting to be helpful, I went into the road and aided cars with pushes. I was called to the Rector's office the next day and scolded for leaving grounds. I diplomatically said I did not agree, this was merely an act of kindness.

In the summers, we returned home. Due to Dad's position as vice president of the steel company in Battle Creek, he 'pulled strings' to get me a job as a vacation replacement worker. I rotated throughout three plants filling in by doing piece-work welding and other jobs. As the Catholic church paid our room, board and tuition, these funds helped pay for the incidentals.

Concerning the tragic and widespread sex abuse scandals among Catholic religious that were exposed in the 1990s and still an issue today, I never witnessed or heard of anything like this in my experiences as an altar server or seminarian. So, I conclude while an awful, multi-year systemic failure of the church to regulate its own, these are isolated incidents. The scope appears huge due to the duration and size of the church around the world.

What I can say, however, is that any kind of scandal is considered a serious threat in the church hierarchy, so there is a natural resistance to publicity causing a lack of transparency. Nevertheless, concealing and not preventing or stopping something as vile as pedophilia is unforgiveable. I did observe at Saint Gregory that priests were assigned there to keep them out of parishes. These may be related mainly to personality difficulties and nothing of a sexual nature. The practice of moving 'bad apples' rather than removing them I do not doubt.

After two years in Cincinnati, our Battle Creek seminarian contingent complained so much about the regimentation to our priests back home, the diocese listened and transferred us to Sacred Heart Seminary in Detroit, Michigan.

SACRED HEART SEMINARY

What a difference! Sacred Heart Seminary was more like a small college. Aside from set classes, there was no daily schedule, no 'Grand Silence', no restrictions on where we could go and little regimentation. We were treated like adults. The priest faculty seemed more friendly and helpful and mature dealing with us.

The seminary is located on West Chicago Blvd. in inner city Detroit. No Black seminarian or faculty resided on campus in neighborhood of mostly Black residents. Our relationship with the community was cordial, however. The seminary employed members of the local community and opened its gym facilities on weekends to let the neighbor kids play basketball.

1967 was an eventful year in Detroit. It exploded in five days of riots in July, one of the most destructive in American history. In streets surrounding our campus, looting and arson was rampant. 8,000 Michigan national guardsman were deployed. Tanks were cruising the streets. We were safe inside in lockdown mode.

On the corner of our grounds at Linwood and Chicago streets, there is a large grotto with a statue of Jesus. On the first night of the riots, someone painted the face and hands black. We were delighted as we were staunch supporters of the Civil Rights Movement. The following night, someone painted it white. We petitioned the seminary rector and he had it repainted black again and it has remained that way until today in solidarity with our neighbors and the large Black community of Detroit.

DIFFICULT DECISION

The summer of 1968 was one of personal turmoil as I struggled with the idea of not returning for senior year at the seminary. What was gnawing at me for at least a year was if I was truly cut-out for the single life. It was not about religion or celibacy, but a matter of lifestyle. Saint Gregory was so intensely regimented I suppressed such thoughts; yet freedom at Sacred Heart and summer vacations gave me space to challenge my true feelings. Perhaps being a twin made me value companionship, but I came to a tearful and cathartic decision to end my life-long aspirations about the priesthood deciding not to return to Sacred Heart. I had a heart-to-heart meeting with my vocation director who was empathetic and honored by decision. I was grateful.

WESTERN MICHIGAN UNIVERSITY

I never regretted that decision. Yet, that led to anxiety about what lies ahead. I was staring at a blank page about my future. All

I knew for sure was I was still altruistic and a people person. So, I decided medicine would be a wise direction. Working at Dad's factory during the summer of 1968, I earned enough to pay tuition for the first time. I enrolled at Western Michigan University (WMU) in Kalamazoo, about twenty miles west of Battle Creek. Among the classes I signed up for were chemistry and physics beginning the Fall semester.

A high school classmate was living in an apartment near the WMU campus and told me the next-door apartment was available, so I moved there and my new life at a secular university began. Still naïve about women, I kept a low profile while attending coed classes for the first time at the university level.

What became all too clear was I could not master chemistry nor physics. Either for lack of interest or smarts, I decided I was not meant for science or medicine. Frustrated that I wasted a semester, I decided to complete my original major, Philosophy, to get my bachelor's degree. I knew that degree was not useful, but I wanted to complete it regardless. To my delight, my WMU counselor examined my transcript and advised I had enough Latin credits to declare it as my required minor subject without further courses. So, I completed the additional philosophy course work and other requirements and graduated from WMU in 1970.

Needing funds to survive during the terms, I found work at a McDonald's where my neighbor and former classmate was working. Unbelievably, the name of the franchise owner and manager was Mickey McDonald. After interviewing me and noticing I was a 'people person', he assigned me to the front window to take and fulfill customer orders. So, it was classes in the daytime and work at McDonald's in the evenings.

I befriended fellow McDonalds staff. At that time only boys or men worked in McDonalds. Of course, I was comfortable with this. Barney, Arch, Terry, and I decided to find and share a two-bedroom apartment near the university. We got along very well. Terry was dating Martha, the daughter of the Borgess Hospital CEO, Martin Verzi, a 450-bed medical center near our McDonalds. As it turned out, Martha became pregnant by mistake and Terry must have felt obligated to marry her, so he proposed to Martha.

NIGHT HOUSE ORDERLY

I was in Terry's wedding party when I met Mr. Verzi, Martha's father. We chatted. He learned I was finishing my degree and asked if I would like to work at the hospital. I said absolutely if I could coordinate with classes. I interviewed for and was accepted into the next hospital orderly training program. After several weeks training in orderly tasks including placing catheters, giving enemas, learning CPR, doing vital signs and other bedside chores, I was given a pager and became the hospital's night 'house orderly' which meant I was assigned to a base unit (normally where someone called in sick to be the extra hands), but my main job was to answer my pager and perform orderly work everywhere in this five-story, three wing complex. They trained me to do 'stat' or immediate EKGs. I had no idea then that this experience would change my life dramatically in the future. I left Borgess with an exemplary work record.

Still without a direction after graduating with a BA degree, I pondered my future. Early in my final year at WMU, I considered entering the Peace Corps, Teacher Corps or Vista Volunteers. All were actively recruiting. Comparing these, I favored the Teacher Corps because it would include a tuition free master's degree in Education during the two-year commitment. I submitted my application and heard nothing for almost a year.

Unexpected, I receive a letter from the University of Wisconsin about the time of my graduation. They had just been funded for an *Indian Teacher Corps* project involving seven of ten Wisconsin Indian reservations. I was invited to Madison to compete for one of twenty master's degree slots with over two hundred applicants submitted. Twenty-eight bachelor's degree slots would be awarded also. I drove to Wisconsin, met with a large committee of university and Native American community members, and was grilled for about 30 minutes. Perhaps my seminarian background helped, and my interview must have gone well. I was awarded a slot in the University of Wisconsin graduate school. My next two years was spent in Wisconsin. This Detroit Lion fan in me had to grimace and hold my tongue every time I heard obnoxious cries of Green Bay Packer fans that populated northeastern Wisconsin.

VIETNAM WAR

Timing is everything. On December 1, 1969, the *Selective Service System* of the United States conducted lotteries for military service in the Vietnam War. My birthdate landed me number #81 which meant my time was imminent. I was not supportive of the war and consulted a lawyer who recommended

I seek 'conscientious objector' (CO) status based on religious convictions and my time as a seminarian. This status was approved. However, it meant I would be inducted into military service as a medic or another non-combat position. CO status does not exempt someone from serving somehow. With a lottery number of #81, my time for a military physical would come soon.

I enclosed my acceptance letter from the Wisconsin Indian Teacher Corps in a letter sent to the *Selective Service* advising them of this new position in a government funded program and asked them to consider this as my 'alternative service' for draft. They accepted this and so my tour of duty in Wisconsin satisfied my Vietnam War draft obligation. What a relief!

WISCONSIN TEACHER CORPS

Although most Teacher Corps projects are inner city programs, Wisconsin's was directed at uplifting the cultural identities of Native American children by making their school systems near these reservations more respectful of Native American sensibilities in their curriculum designs. So, we Teacher Corps interns were meant to serve as change agents challenging the status quo.

After initial summer classes at the state university in Stevens Point, our class of forty-eight were split-up and assigned to one of seven reservations. I was one of seven interns sent to Bowler Wisconsin Public Schools near to the Stockbridge-Munsee Indian Reservation. Native Americans were about 50% of the student body. Literally, this tribe is the last of the Mohicans, pushed westward from Massachusetts to their final stop in Wisconsin.

This was a K-6 grade project geared at intervention with youngsters. At that time, reservations had no casinos. They were at or near poverty levels economically with high incidences of alcoholism, diabetes, and other social ills. We were highly active. We spent full days in the classroom paired with teachers or given small groups to tutor; we went to the reservation in the evenings to tutor students; and we were active in civic affairs. I was asked to become the Cub Scout Master which I accepted. My two fellow roommates became 'den mothers'. During the school terms, our professors came to visit us as we continued a full course load.

In the intervening summer, we took graduate courses in Madison at the University of Wisconsin. Hotly political protesting against the Vietnam War, I joined marches. We assembled in front of the university library and marched up State Street toward the Capital building. Before too long, authorities were lobbing teargas our way and we scattered to escape the smoke and took alternative routes to get to the Capital building that was surrounded by troops. We did all we could to register our protests peacefully against the Vietnam War.

Returning for our final year of internship in Bowler in the Fall, I wrote a successfully funded federal grant to pay salaries and buy supplies to teach Native American children arts and crafts that their grandparents still could pass on. We paid Native American senior citizens wages to take kids into the forest, pick out certain trees, cut them down, debark, strip, and soak the wood, and then teach them how to construct baskets. Another group taught weaving; another making silver jewelry; and still another, the art of beading.

My last academic step was to write a master's thesis before leaving Bowler and meeting with three professors in Madison to defend my thesis, and then I left Wisconsin proud to have served the Native American community in the Teacher Corps while earning a Master of Science (MS) in *Curriculum & Instruction*. While my fellow interns continued careers in the education, I decided I did not want to remain an elementary teacher. The curriculum did not interest me, and I was as much a surrogate father to kids from broken homes. I did not find this fulfilling. I headed back to Michigan with another life decision to make. At least I was no longer staring at a Vietnam War obligation, and I accomplished something noble over the past two years in Wisconsin.

BATTLE CREEK SANITARIUM

Seeking a new direction, I left Wisconsin for my hometown in Battle Creek. Needing work, I took my orderly credentials to the Battle Creek Sanitarium, and they hired me in their psychiatric hospital. This was the same famous sanitarium that the Kellogg brother's operated year before and made famous. W.K. Kellogg invented cereal flakes and made Battle Creek the "cereal city." Now, the Sanitarium was a psychiatric hospital operated by the Seventh Day Adventist Church.

A practice that I could not abide yet I had to abet against my better judgement was holding patients involuntarily beyond a legal holding period of 72 hours. These were usually patients with substance abuse problems that were now coherent and simply wanted to leave. The nursing station would inform the psychiatrist and sometimes they did not get another court order in time to continue the involuntary hold. We orderlies were stationed at the exit to bar these patients from leaving until they got the new court order. Knowing these patients were coherent and not dangerous, their constitutional rights were being denied after the 72 hours had lapsed and I complained to the head nurse. She ignored me.

The next time this abuse occurred, I was told to stand at the exit and prevent the patient from leaving. Instead, I let the person out. I walked to the head nurse office, put down my keys and said, "I quit". She said, "good that you did, because I would have fired you for insubordination." I left feeling righteous about my action.

Fortunately, weeks before this incident, Borgess Hospital contacted me after more than two years and asked if I would return to my orderly duties there. They needed more staff. I agreed. Meanwhile, I came to a decision that a master's degree in Counseling would be a good complimentary degree to my MS in Education. I could become a school counselor. So, as I was preparing to return to Kalamazoo, I inquired and enrolled into the Counseling & Personnel master's degree program at WMU.

BORGESS HOSPITAL

Trying to juggle evening graduate courses at WMU and pay for my education, I resumed my job as night 'house orderly'. I slept in the daytime. After about one year of service, I was ready to leave after a night shift ended at 7 A.M., Lilian Martin approached me. I had not met her before. She was director of the hospital's Unit Manager program. She asked if I had interested in this type of position. This would be an incredible promotion which would not conflict with my courses. She said she had offered the newly opened position to someone else but would consider me for that or future opening. I readily agreed and thanked her. Soon thereafter, Lilian approached me again to inform me another person accepted that position, but her position was now available in the nurse staffing office and Lilian offered me that position. Again, it sounded interesting and did not conflict with WMU, so I accepted. Now, I could sleep at night, work in the days, and attend classes in the evening.

NURSE STAFFING COORDINATOR

There was only three of us in this office: Ellie, the director, Bobbi, and me. I prepared monthly schedules for all the RNs and LPNs. Tedious work but I enjoyed it. Using a template and a pencil, I prepared for each nurse their monthly schedule factoring in vacations and making sure weekends and all units were covered. Much communicating with nursing staff was involved. Bobbi's job was to call in help to cover illnesses or absences each day. Ellie monitored everything and if staffing became critical, she had authority to offer double pay in a pinch. We were a good team.

UNIT MANAGER

In less than a year, another *Unit Manager* position opened, and Lilian followed up on her promise and offered me the position. I was nearing completion of my degree work at WMU, so this worked out well. I was paired with a head nurse on three units. My role involved supervising the ward clerks, managing all non-clinical matters including supplies, housekeeping, maintenance, and listening and resolving family complaints. I worked in the position for a year when a new opportunity arose.

Rumors were circulating that Dr. James McCarthy, Director of Trauma and Ambulatory Services, was looking for an assistant director. His areas were beginning major expansion programs and considering his part-time clinical role and love of golfing, he did not want to get too mired into construction matters. I interviewed with Dr. McCarthy and was again promoted.

I had enjoyed each position at Borgess and this was no exception. With blueprints sprawled on my desk, I identified all fixed equipment needed in all areas from clinic rooms, ER surgical suites to waiting rooms; and then worked with the purchasing department to order everything and with maintenance for installations. I worked with the medical and nursing leaders Pediatrics, Oncology, Nephrology, Cardiac Rehab to keep the ambulatory units properly staffed, equipped, and supplied.

After these outpatient constructions projects were completed and dedications held, Dr. McCarthy decided to leave Borgess. He recommended to Mr. Verzi that I become the new Director. This only required shuttling his clinical duties to another doctor. Otherwise, he assured the CEO that I could manage these new responsibilities.

DIRECTOR OF TRAUMA AND AMBULATORY CARE

I was now a member of senior management at Borgess reporting to the CEO, Mr. Verzi, the same retired Army colonel who had offered me a position just years earlier at Martha's wedding. I did not want or need an assistant as I faced exciting challenges in my new position

At that time, Kalamazoo had only basic EMT private and volunteer ambulance services. Mr. Verzi's proudest accomplishments were recruiting subspecialties to the Kalamazoo area. These included cardiology, neurology and neurosurgery, nephrology, and oncology. It was time for Kalamazoo to provide advanced paramedic services to support these services. I collaborated with my counterpart at the other hospital in Kalamazoo and the city's Fire Chief. We planned and introduced the area's first paramedic service. The hospitals provided training and medical supervision, and the Fire Dept. had the workforce and paramedic units.

With more attention paid to subspecialties, there was a growing need for family physicians in our area. And so, we devoted a wing of our ambulatory care building to initiate a Family Practice Residency Program adding this to the residency programs already existing in orthopedics, pediatrics, and internal medicine. We hired a Family Practice Residency Director and I collaborated with him to organize and staff the new Family Practice ambulatory center.

U.S. hospitals have a major hurdle every three years. That is an accreditation inspection from the *Joint Commission (JCAHO)*. Borgess was due for its next accreditation. Former Army Colonel

Verzi knew all about inspections; this was serious business. And I resolved that my areas would be prepared. Each area had accreditation standards including policies, procedures and documentation showing that all vital areas of operations are functioning properly. I worked diligently with all my departments to be ready.

Finally, the week of JC inspection came with a commission team of a doctor, a nurse, and an administrator. They toured every nook of the hospital, talked with staff everywhere, and reviewed piles of documents. At the end of the visit, the team presented verbal finding in front of the management team in the hospital auditorium. When they came my areas of responsibility, the remarks were glowing. The administrator said he had not seen such a well-run operation for quite some time. Of course, I was glowing inside. And I could tell Colonel Verzi was pleased. Borgess got its full three-year accreditation.

In mid-1977, before I turned twenty-nine, Mr. Verzi called me to his office and told me he wanted to recommend me for the new CEO position that opened at Dowagiac's Lee Memorial Hospital. I was stunned and of course delighted. I went for an interview with the Lee Memorial Board of Trustees, and they offered me the position, largely on Mr. Verzi's recommendation. Without the appropriate graduate degree, which is a typical requirement for a healthcare executive, I embarked on what was to become my career in healthcare executive leadership. I finally found my niche.

LEE MEMORIAL HOSPITAL

Like Gulliver's travels, I moved from an urban hospital of 450 beds to a rural hospital of seventy-five beds. Yet, the basics were all there: med-surg units, ICU, lab, radiology, medical records, quality assurance, respiratory, PT, pharmacy, housekeeping, maintenance, boiler, and back-up generator with underground fuel tanks, ER, surgery, helicopter pad and cafeteria. And of course, an independent medical staff that needed to me managed and catered to.

I will relay three challenges I faced while in Dowagiac. First, when I arrived, the physical plant had just begun a major expansion program that doubled the square footage of the
hospital's footprint and included remodeling all the older areas. Virtually every department had to be relocated in the process, so the logistics planning was extensive. We managed through this coordination and had a wonderful open house, and this rural community was proudly served in a new facility. As the largest employer with 250 full time equivalents, the hospital was an important institution in Dowagiac and Cass County.

Secondly, medical staff recruitment is often a major challenge in rural areas and Cass County was no exception. If fact, the area was federally designated as a medical workforce shortage area. This meant we qualified for federal grants to support recruitment and operations of clinic in our area. We recruited National Health Service Corps physician scholarship recipients who were required to serve in such medical workforce shortage areas to repay their scholarship loans. I wrote the grant for our area and was able to staff clinics to our east and north where no family physicians had been before. I also recruited the areas first OB/GYN and added to our internal medicine staff.

Thirdly, I knew my CEO position in Dowagiac might be my last without the appropriate graduate degree. Fortunately, the *University of Michigan Public Health School* had an on-job/on-campus program that conferred master's degrees in public health (MPH) with a concentration on running medical care organizations. I applied and was accepted into a class of about forty students including doctors, nurses and dentists pursing an MPH. For two years, I commuted 140 miles monthly to Ann Arbor, Thursday to Sunday. The same professors that taught the on-campus graduate students repeated these lectures in back-to-back sessions for the four days. In 1982, I finished these courses and was awarded my MPH, my third graduate degree. It was not soon thereafter that my next opportunity emerged. Finally, my prolonged academic career was over.

SSJ HEALTH SYSTEM

In 1983, the Congregation of the Sisters of St. Joseph of Nazareth who were the sponsors of seven Michigan hospitals including Lee Memorial decided to create a health system office in Kalamazoo at their motherhouse to better coordinate sponsorship and governance of their hospitals. A former president of the congregation, Sister Irene, was appointed president of this new health system corporation. She had a Ph.D. in English and was an educator, so we wanted someone with healthcare management expertise as her Senior Vice President. She was on my Board of Trustees; she knew I was capable and offered the position to me.

I bid farewell to the staff in Dowagiac and moved back to Kalamazoo. I was no longer dealing with day-to-day hospital operations, but with health systems management. We had a modest staff, so I performed executive functions that are sometimes split. For example, with no chief financial officer, I received from all the hospitals' monthly financial statements and prepared monthly consolidated statement and presented them at our board meetings. I helped plan and coordinate an annual strategic planning event that determined what programs we would combine at a system level. I established and operated a senior citizen marketing program offered at all our hospitals. This outreach program served over 100,000 seniors in Michigan. Similar in concept to an airline's frequent flyer loyalty program, it offered services for senior such as free valet parking, discounts for outpatient medicines, medical lectures, and quarterly newsletters.

One area requiring system coordination was Risk Management. Our Michigan hospitals formed two offshore captive insurance companies in the Cayman Islands. This was a vehicle for funding expenses related to medical malpractice claims. Lawful, it allowed hospitals to put money into Cayman banks and avoid paying U.S. federal taxes on investment proceeds. This tax reduction meant more funds would pay actual expenses. As indemnity companies, we managed insurance claims within the U.S. but we had to go outside the U.S. to operate the captives. We normally had one annual meetings in the Cayman Islands and all other meetings in Windsor, Ontario. I chaired the onshore insurance committee where we reviewed cases, set reserves, and managed the lawyers who were assigned cases.

Around 1990, the system office moved to Ann Arbor, Michigan. Sister Irene retired and a new President was appointed who I served in the same capacity. The new president was a former president of the sister's Nazareth College without a healthcare background and so he was pleased to have my expertise.

Around 1989, the congregations of the Sisters of St. Joseph and the Daughters of Charity began to discuss a possible merge of their respective health systems. The next year was a period of intense negotiations, planning and execution of this merger.

In the seventies, Catholic religious congregations recognized that with their numbers of religious dwindling and average age of nuns increasing, their ability to sponsor and govern major healthcare institutions across the country would become challenging. Gradually, they began to fill board and management positions with lay persons. In addition, to consolidate governance, they began to creating health system offices to consolidate control over institutions and take advantages of greater economies of scale such as in finance and purchasing to better steward these non-profit assets.

The two religious congregations agreed on essential matters and gave our executive teams the responsibility to work out details of the merger. I was appointed *Transition Manager* for SSJ Health System and was paired with a counterpart at the Daughters of Charity National Health system. Over months, we formed and orchestrated committees composed of senior executives from both systems to address key issues involving governance, finance, corporate headquarters, HR benefits, risk management issues and more. Our work competed, the sisters approved the committee reports and were ready to bless a newly merged entity.

ASCENSION HEALTH

The merged system, *Ascension Health*, began operations in 1999 at its corporate headquarters in St. Louis, MO. The system began with sixty-five hospitals in twenty-five states with over 100,000 employees. I was offered and accepted the new positions of Senior Vice President and Corporate Responsibility Officer.

My portfolio included risk management, human resources, facilities management, and corporate responsibility. The following are major challenges I faced at Ascension Health during my tenure.

As the system Corporate Responsibility Officer (CRO), I designed and implemented the new corporate-wide program. This required we appoint a CRO in each hospital who reported to me. We then published our program details which explained to all employees their responsibilities to perform ethically and in accord with our values. All current employees were given brochures to read and sign acceptance forms. All new employees were introduced to the program during orientation. An anonymous hotline number was established for employees who felt they could not go directly to their supervisors. And a system-wide information data base was created to track, and monitor issued raised until resolved.

Risk Management continued to be an area of my expertise. We now had three offshore captive insurance companies. The Vice President of Risk Management reported to me. I continued to oversee these operations for years. Regarding Human Resources, a major problem was our pension program. The other health system prior to the merger had spent years trying to install a new IT software without success and at great expense.

My challenge was to diagnose and fix this problem. I decided the director of pension services had to go and we needed to find a replacement IT system. I fired that director and hired a major HR consultant to find the best IT solution. We found a vendor with state-of-the-art pension system to outsource with. I hired a new pension services director who was able to convert the old system onto the vendor IT platform and the program stabilized.

With the World Wide Web beginning to make itself useful in a corporate setting, I contracted with an E-leaning software vendor to put our compliance training program online. This successful install required that all 100,000+ employees sign-in and take on-line courses. A tracking mechanism allowed HR departments to monitor performance. Employees had to successfully complete the course to be eligible for their next salary increase.

By 2008, my healthcare executive career spanning thirty years was ending. I retired and moved to Thailand to begin a next chapter of my life. I was truly thankful to have a wonderful career.

PERSPECTIVES

MY LIFE, TIMES & CONVICTIONS

CHAPTER III

RELIGION & SPIRITUALITY RECONSIDERED

CONTENTS

Preface 55
Language 56
Cults 59
Accidents 60
Immortality 60
Ignorance 63
Infallibility 64
Humility 65
Cosmology 66
Philosophy 66
Psychology 68
Church and State 71
Scandal 74
Zealotry 74
Afterword 75

PREFACE

When I make the following distinction, I am not trying to be cute or trite: we are human beings; we are not spiritual beings. To be precise, we are human beings endowed with a spiritual dimension. This is not splitting hairs. Spirituality is enabled by our humanity.

G. K. Chesterton (1874 - 1936), the English writer and philosopher, said the poet puts his mind into the heavens and the mathematician puts the heavens into his mind. He artfully described the scope and ingenuity of our minds. Our mentality begets spirituality. If there is a theme in this book, this is it.

Spirituality and religion concern critical and sensitive aspects of meaning and purpose in our lives and are often central to family or communal experiences.

To be clear at the outset, let me differentiate spirituality from religion. Spirituality requires belief in transcendental or supernatural life beyond our immediate human experience. We associate this with a *soul* distinct from and believed to survive outside our body after death.

Spirituality is the overarching framework within which religions reside each with established doctrines and structures of authority. Large percentages of world population adhere to two major religions: Christianity and Islam. The remaining percentages are subdivided into over fifteen other known religions including Judaism, Buddhism and Hinduism.

Whatever spiritual or religious beliefs we are born into and raised, most accept these beliefs unconditionally without questioning and many of us pass these on to our children as if it were a native tongue or spiritual DNA.

This was true in my case. A devout Roman Catholic, my mother was raised by Polish parents who settled around 1900 into a small town in SW Michigan from Chicago. The town had a large Polish community. The parish, the rosary and polka parties enjoyed on Saturday nights in the parish hall were core to her identity. Mother carried her faith to her grave and instilled it in her five children. After high school, I left home to enter freshman year in a seminary in Cincinnati to become a Catholic priest.

I remember my mother remarking, "Jackie (my nickname then) loves to take things apart and see how they tick." I carried this innate inquisitiveness throughout my life. After seventy years, my search for meaning brought me to a vastly different place from where I left home.

LANGUAGE

A good place to begin a reconsideration of spirituality and religious meaning is by framing it as a uniquely human quest for meaning. I believe language is the foundation of meaning.

I recall in *Philosophy 101*, Plato's 'allegory of the cave' Plato postulated that humans only see mere reflections of reality, as if facing a cave wall, able only to observe shadows and never able to turn around to see the actual or real objects themselves. The real objects were Plato's *world of forms or ideas*. He literally believed this world of forms or ideas were what was real, timeless, absolute, unchangeable.

While I reject Plato's argument about reality and its implications, I find one extremely useful insight in the allegory of the cave: the paramount importance of ideas in human history. We need go no further than *Wikipedia* to obtain an elegant definition of *ideation* as 'the creative process of generating, developing and communicating innovative ideas, where an idea is understood as a basic element of thought.'

Naturally, our fabulous innate linguistic capacity in concert with our senses and imagination enabled ideation. The development of language about 50,000 years ago may have happened something like this: our ancestral hunters and gathers began to name plants they encountered. Some were edible and some poisonous so there was some urgency to classify these plants and share this lexicon and knowledge with the clan. In this simple example, we may discern the dawning of language, development of a body of ideas and knowledge through discovery (learning), science (botany and taxonomy) and education (teaching).

Human's linguistic and physiological endowments underpinned and enabled a growing sophistication in coping with their environment and dominating lesser species and the world at large. Oral language development was a necessary condition for heightened awareness, introspection, imagination, and communication. Between 3,500 BC and 3,000 BC, the ancient

Sumerians are credited for inventing writing which rendered language an even more potent instrument of human progress.

Words bestow and convey, symbolically and phonetically, meaning and awareness of persons, places, things, techniques, events, phenomena, impressions, sensibilities, attitudes, concepts, etc. Whether rudimentary utterances like 'Ma' or complex terms of astrophysics that came later, language facilitates exercise of our cerebral gifts accounting for humanity's extraordinary dominance on planet Earth.

Likewise, spiritual ideation and lexicon arose from linguistic genius. Language was obviously critical to tame, survive and thrive in their harsh environments, but how did language spawn the spiritual realm of consciousness? I suspect when early humans could afford time for contemplation, be attentive to the mysteries of life beyond their grasp, express gratitude or awe, and appeal for good fortune, they created polytheism to harness these impulses. Expressions of spirituality through songs, chants, myths as well as dance and art become as important to them as daily toil. All the essential elements of culture that emerged.

7,000 known languages are now extant. Novel words are created within each lexicon every day and dialects undergo constant adaptation. The English of Chaucer is vastly different from the English of Shakespeare, or of Hemingway. British and US English are becoming increasingly distinctive. The English lexicon alone has over a million words.

Humans have two fundamental orientations: to manipulate and to appreciate. Languages are symbolic cerebral manipulations that allow us to conceptualize, understand and focus. Vocal cords facilitate phonetics enabling discourse.

CULTS

The word "cult" is often viewed with derision as an affront to mainstream religions. Yet it is the root of the word "culture". Many of us associate the word with paganism or Jim Jones' *Peoples Temple* or the *Branch Davidians*.

If you were an ancient upper class Roman citizen enjoying status, material wealth and the 'good life' and someone accused you of 'being a pagan', this was meant as a biting insult and indictment. It insinuated your beliefs and form of worship were invalid, nonsense and a sacrilege. You would certainly be offended. And if you were told that 'monotheism' was the only true form of divinity, you might be incensed, and not in a liturgical sense.

If you step back and embrace this historic scenario with perspective and empathy, you can discern the difference between a 'cult' and a 'religion'; that is, 'critical mass'. When a sufficient portion of a community accepts as legitimate a set of beliefs, a tipping point is reached where any blurring between cult and religion recedes, and the community clearly recognizes and validates those beliefs as a religion. Using a metaphor from entomology, a cult may be the 'cocoon stage' of a religion.

Cults morph into religion through ubiquitous adoption. Early Christians in meager numbers immediately after Christ left his disciples were considered an odd Jewish cult. In time, through conversions, perseverance, persecutions, good works, 'critical mass' propelled most Romans to becoming Christian. Christianity moved from the fringes of society to become the central religion in that part of the world.

ACCIDENTS

What a particular person comes to believe in the spiritual or religious realm is determined largely by accident of location. A rational person must concede that if they were born in Pakistan today, rather than in the USA, they would highly likely be a Muslim, not Christian. Location, location, location.

The next obvious accidental determinant is parental authority and beliefs. I was born into a Roman Catholic family. My boyfriend next door was born into a Jewish family. These accidental determents suggest it may be arrogant to declare one religion superior even though we might favor the one we happen to practice.

As we mature, innumerable life experiences nudge or thrust us into validating or reconsidering our spiritual or religious beliefs. Who we meet, what we study, what and who we encounter, places we go, and our health can influence what we believe. I consider these accidental determinants, not preordained.

IMMORTALITY

The fear, pain, loss, grief, and mystery associated with death is one of the most perplexing existential questions and concerns of the human condition. Whoever first suggested the comforting notion of an immortal human soul is unknown, but they must have enjoyed instant popularity. Whether in myth or religion, belief in immortality has ameliorated the sting of death for many over millennia.

The conviction and comfort derived from this belief is extremely difficult to shake or displace. I recall while serving as an altar server at funerals in my local parish how consolation was derived by the words of scripture promising eternal life and reunion with those we love. And belief in immortality is not exclusively found in religious doctrine; it is a widely held spiritual tenet.

Personally, my initial pondering of immortality was never meant as an afront against religious doctrine; it was triggered by two nagging questions of 'plausibility' and 'necessity'. Consequently, I came to the conviction that our human existence will end, in all respects, at the moment of physical death. It is not an easy conclusion to reach, I admit. Losing such comfort is disconcerting.

My argument concerning plausibility begins with the popular definition of the essence of human nature as the composite of 'mind-body-spirit' ('spirit' sometimes called the 'soul'). The crux of this argument is this composite we describe as three discreet components are, in fact, inseparable, not divisible.

Life depends on the integrity of this unity. Determined by absence of cardiac and respiratory functions and sometimes associated with 'brain death', the integrity of this mind-body-spirit unity collapses at moment of death.

I reject the belief that some spiritual release occurs by which the soul exits a decedent and sustains independent life and consciousness -- which neuroscientists refer to as the province of the upper brain. And this rejection extends to beliefs in the reunion of soul with body later, or in reincarnation or transmigration.

In terms of necessity, am I satisfied living this life only? Yes. Do I personally need an eternal heavenly reward or threat of hell to comfort, motivate or deter me? No. Does this change the way I should or would conduct my life? No. Can I accept this same fate for those I love? Yes. Am I upset I will not see my loved ones after death? If it were plausible, yes; but I have faced that grim reality. So, no. I better make the best of it now...tell them "I love them" and treat them with TLC while I am able, and then let fond memories sustain us after we part ways.

And why is it necessary than humans are singled out for this incredible advantage of immortality over other mammals or any other matter. Not even our sun will enjoy immortality. In roughly five billion years, the sun will run out of energy.

Had Jesus told his disciples he was divine, but they were mere mortals and not rewarded with supernatural or eternal life, would Christianity still have flourished? Certainly, Christian text and doctrine would need dramatic revisions. Yet, would the teachings and examples of Jesus in the *New Testament* exhorting and inspiring followers to live a life of love, charity, communion, sacrifice, and gratitude hold firm absent the promise of eternal bliss. Our rewards would be our own peace of mind and knowing we have made a positive impact on the lives of others. Had the notion of immortality never entered human consciousness, I suspect spirituality and religious practices could have flourished, nonetheless.

The brilliant cosmologist Carl Sagan said, *"I would love to believe that when I die I will live again, that some thinking, feeling, remembering part of me will continue. But as much as I want to believe that, and despite the ancient and worldwide cultural traditions that assert an afterlife, I know of nothing to suggest that it is more than wishful thinking."* (Carl Sagan, "Billions & Billions: Thoughts on Life and Death at the Brink of the Millennium").

IGNORANCE

Fervent believers and those entrusted to protect religious orthodoxy sometimes abhor anyone who abandons their faith, toys with and succumb to contrary beliefs. Apostasy and heresy were severe offenses deserving of disdain and censure.

Historically, a favorite tactic for limiting the risk of desertion was imposing or maintaining mass ignorance. In the *Middle Ages*, the only educated and literate were clergy and segments of the royal and elite classes. Keeping the masses illiterate and ignorant was ideal for maintaining orthodoxy, creating mystique, and nipping any tendency for rebellion. Silencing contrary views and their dissemination sustained ignorance. Ignorance is bliss, they contend.

This tactic is just as potent in the 21st Century. I cite three contemporary examples:

1) We cringe when we see the Taliban of Afghanistan -- motivated by a distorted radical view of Islam -- barring teenage girls from school, keeping them ignorant and submissive.

2) The Turkish government recently introduced what they call a 'values-based curriculum' prohibiting teaching of evolution. This hearkens back to 1925 when high school teacher, John T. Scopes, was accused of violating the *Tennessee's Butler Act* in which state-funded schools were not permitted by law to teach human evolution in any state-funded school.

3) Strict controls on the internet, news outlets and social media is practiced today by theocratic and totalitarian governments to repress and stifle independent, critical thinking and commentary.

INFALLIBILITY

One corrosive religious edict deployed sometimes is a declaration of infallibility, the inability to be wrong. In Western culture, this is most notable in the Catholic doctrine on papal infallibility; an effective instrument for impeding dialogue, discouraging dissent, promoting orthodoxy and unconditional acceptance. Regrettably, it has proven damaging as it institutionalizes stubbornness and resistance to consider new information or circumstances. A clear example is the church's stance rejecting contraception as an unwelcome challenge to natural law and theological arguments that seems absurdly deficient in the face of population growth. They continue to promote the naïvely insufficient solutions of abstinence and rhythm and reject sensible solutions like condoms.

HUMILITY

My favorite definition of humility is 'knowing your place and taking it'. In the grand scheme of things, consider that our solar system has nine planets while our Milky Way has an estimated four hundred million planets. The number of planets estimated in the observable universe is extraordinarily huge. Given that 'homo sapiens' arrived extremely late by earth's cosmic clock, and the chances of our replicating on another planet slim, humility suggests we recognize we inhabit a relatively puny nook in the cosmos and have for a relatively brief timespan.

Nonetheless, religious traditions have espoused an outsized role for humanity within our universe. It was not that long ago in human history that a core tenet of religious faith was that planet Earth was the center of divine creation. When science challenged this article of belief, the church objected and stifled discussion out of hubris, not humility.

COSMOLOGY

Cosmology, the branch of astronomy concerned with the study of the origin and chronology of the universe, was a fundamental focus of early Catholic theological discourse. Thomas Aquinas (1225-1274), one of the most consequential Catholic theologians, concluded that it was necessary to arrive at a 'first mover' of the cosmos, moved by no other; and this first mover he understood to be God.

Could not someone with no spiritual orientation also declare there must be a 'first mover' that was the originator of the 'Big Bang' creating our vast and unfolding universe of mass and energy with all its mystery, complexity, and majesty? That person might not call this 'first mover' *God*, and yet acknowledge this incredible source or force that was responsible while expressing awe and gratitude that this 'first mover' created and put into motion the stardust from which the Earth and we were born. Is not this conviction without a theology just as valid?

PHILOSOPHY

Greek philosophy was a bedrock of human knowledge in Western civilization. The early Greek philosophers include Thales, Anaximander, Heraclitus, and Pythagoras. Later came the classic Greek philosophers Socrates, Plato, and Aristotle.

The word 'philosophy' comes from the Greek *philo* (love) and *sophia* (wisdom). If you review a college curriculum for a philosophy major today, you will notice it covers a vast swath of what later became discreet academic pursuits and professions.

These include astronomy, mathematics, politics, ethics, law, architecture, medicine, and metaphysics akin to religious studies.

Much of this accumulated wisdom was lost in the West during the so-called "Dark Middle Ages" and led to a period of intellectual and cultural decline extending from about 500-1500 A.D. When these classical Greek sources emerged from the East and rediscovered, it sparked the Renaissance throughout the 15th and 16th centuries.

The influence of ancient Greek philosophers on Christian theology was immense. The two prominent Catholic theologians were ardent students of Greek philosophy. Augustine of Hippo (354 – 430) drew deeply from concepts authored by Plato. Thomas Aquinas was greatly influenced by Aristotle. Portions of Catholic doctrine was rejected in the English and Protestant Reformations in the 16th century. Yet tenets of Christian faith formulated by these earlier theologians held firm, among them the Incarnation, Resurrection and Ascension of Jesus Christ and Doctrine of the Trinity.

Systems of belief are classified by the suffix "ism" including Catholicism, Protestantism, Judaism, and Islamism. The list below are other "isms", that have had profound impact on the world.

AGNOSTICISM--we can know nothing beyond material phenomena.
ASCETICISM--self-denial permits spiritual enlightenment.
CAPITALISM--private ownership/free markets govern economies.
COMMUNISM--classless society/individuals cannot own property.
CONFUCIANISM--system of thought, ethics, and behavior.
EXISTENTIALISM--individual human responsibility.
FASCISM--authoritarian, dictatorial power, forcible suppression.

FATALISM--events are fixed and humans are powerless.
HEDONISM--belief that pleasure is the highest good.
NATURALISM--world can be explained in terms of natural forces.
NIHILISM--denial of all reality; extreme skepticism.
RACISM--belief that race is the primary determinant.
SEXISM--belief in systematic inequalities between the sexes
SOCIALISM--centralized state controls wealth and property.
STOICISM--belief in indifference to pleasure or pain.
THEISM--belief in God without special revelation.
UTILITARIANISM--belief that utility of actions determines moral value.

PSYCHOLOGY

Psychology, the social science that strives to comprehend behavior of individuals offers a means to gain self-awareness and to understand and appreciate the human condition.

When I entered the master's degree program in *Counseling & Personnel* at Western Michigan University in 1974, three distinct tracks of psychological theory were offered in the curriculum, each leading to different approaches to intervention for a counselor to deploy when working with clients. These psychological theories were Freudianism, Behaviorism and Existentialism. We were encouraged to select one and perfect counselling skills consistent with the chosen theory.

While each theory has its merits, I considered existential psychology far more insightful in explaining human behavior, and potentially a more effective way to counsel clients. In pursuing this approach, it had a profound impact on my views on spirituality. In describing this approach, you will readily see how deeply rooted existentialism -- and its therapeutic application -- is in biology and not spirituality, and how religion can disrupt our ability to cope with life.

Danish philosopher Soren Kierkegaard (1813–55) is commonly referred to as the "Father of Existentialism." His philosophy entered the realm of psychology through the works of Rolo May, William James, Viktor Frankl and Abraham Maslow and others.

As existential principles apply to counseling, I admired Frederick S. Perls. M.D., Ph.D. (1893 – 1970), the originator and developer of *Gestalt Therapy*. Perls fled Nazi Germany to South Africa to practice psychiatry and psychoanalysis. I consider Fritz and his wife, Laura, also an accomplished psychotherapist, as most underrated of original thinkers about human nature and therapeutic interventions.

In his first book, *Ego, Hunger and Aggression* (1947), Perls debunked significant portions of Freudianism such as the importance of libido, or sexual instinct, to explain aggression. The following will demonstrate how Perls took his own theory of aggression and applied it to therapy.

Perls believed aggression was centered in the jaws, not the genitals. We bite and chew to digest and assimilate food. This innate aggression is essential to satisfy our hunger and avoid starvation. He saw how integrated this biological reality was when applied to psychology. Gritting your jaws and teeth or yelling are examples of the aggressive emotion we call anger.

How did he apply this to therapy? An example is dealing with resentment which is unexpressed anger. When Perls saw a patient "stuck" in resentment, unable to express anger and deal with it, he called this an 'impasse'. His therapy was directed to help his patients recognize their impasses, help them discover how to channel the excitement of repressed emotions like anger to mobilize their internal resources to deal with them. The goal of this therapy was to prod patients to mature by discovering how to cope, deal with avoidances. He did not coddle patients. It was a time for personal growth, not dependency.

As I delved deeper into existential philosophy and Gestalt psychology, I noticed how these principles seem to be at odds with Western religious concepts. Eastern spirituality was far more compatible, such as Buddhist meditation, even though Kierkegaard was a Lutheran.

Existentialism and Gestalt psychology is based on the principle of "holism". That is, the whole being greater than the sum of its parts. It stresses the integrity of the whole and rejects of the notion that this essential union of 'mind-body-spirit' will somehow separate at death, a contrary notion to holism.

Gestalt espouses the existential principle of the "here and now"; the only time and place to get a patient to address immediate concerns (their "impasse") -- and disrupt their tendency to avoid reality. Therapists use awareness techniques to get patients into the "here and now". For example, anxiety is the stress caused by projecting from the here to then, like stage-fright, anticipating failure. Getting into the 'here and now' through attention to our immediate breathing can dispel anxiety and that excitement can be channeled into productive activity.

Gestalt therapy only asks questions of 'what' and 'how', not 'why'. There is no room for rationalizing in this therapy -- the huge mistake of Freud's that kept his patients on a couch for months and sometimes years. Perls said, "lose your mind and come to your senses". An example of this is in dealing with grief. Some people avoid the pain of grieving and need help -- another type of "impasse". Grief requires feeling (sensing) the psychic pain of loss that triggers the natural emotional response of tears. This is the way through this impasse to find closure and regain balance. This avoidance is a form of neurosis; a healthy person can grieve.

When someone spends their energy trying to get answer to "WHY?" or "WHY ME?" by seeking religious rationalizations, these impede and delay the natural, healthy way to reach closure, acceptance, and cope with life.

CHURCH AND STATE

This chapter discusses religion in the United States. Thomas Jefferson is credited with originating the idea of separation between church and state when he sent a letter to calm the fears of the Baptists of Danbury, Connecticut in 1802. Had Jefferson made only this one contribution to our country -- a concept now enshrined in the First Amendment of the U.S. Constitution -- he would have deserved glowing accolades for all future generations.

Consider the magnitude of the religious and political turmoil the U.S. could have suffered given it is the most heterogeneous population on Earth having welcomed millions of immigrants of multiple faith traditions to its shores. While it is reasonable to assume potential immigrants would never have come if the USA had declared a state religion; nevertheless, it may have been considered a lesser of two evils if present circumstances were intolerable. The consequences of the explosive combination of a state religion, freedom of speech, freedom of assembly and the right to bear arms is daunting even to imagine.

The graphs presented next are published by *Public Religion Research Institute* depict another compounding factor had U.S. declared a state religion: the growth of non-religious.

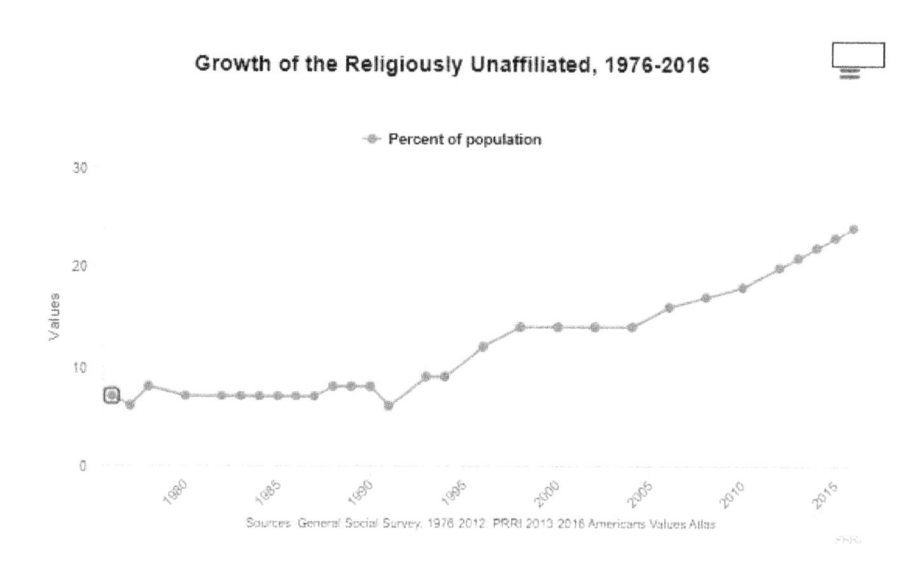

Growth of the Religiously Unaffiliated, 1976-2016

Sources: General Social Survey, 1976-2012; PRRI 2013-2016 Americans Values Atlas

Percent Unaffiliated by Age

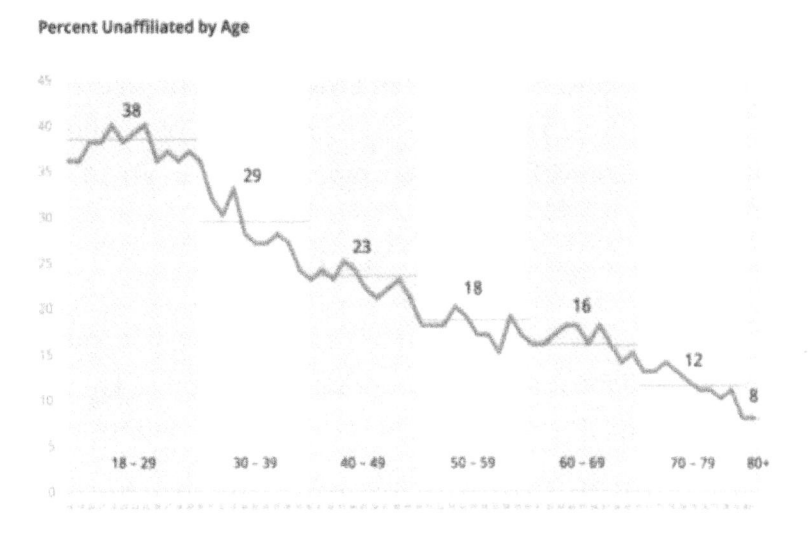

[Line chart showing percent unaffiliated by age group: 18-29: 38, 30-39: 29, 40-49: 23, 50-59: 18, 60-69: 16, 70-79: 12, 80+: 8]

We should not be naïve and underestimate the potency of a coalition of church and state, however. Recent events in the USA demonstrate what can happen when large cohort of religious bond with a political leader. Sadly, while the Covid-19 pandemic ravages the world, the U.S. -- with its copious quantities of vaccines – has been unable to vaccinate believers who accept spurious claims from leaders or the media and have religious convictions contrary to science. The net effect is the entire country suffered lives lost unnecessarily.

While this is an unsavory incident in church – state relationship, there are laudable examples. Among these are *Quakers* who were early abolitionists and other Christians who rallied to end the blight of slavery and later in the civil rights movement led by the Reverend Martin Luther King Jr. in the 50s and 60s.

Another notable example of religious influence on secular governmental was by the *Women's Christian Temperance Union (WCTU)* who vigorously promoted enactment 18th Amendment of the U.S. Constitution established the prohibition of alcohol ratified by January 1919 and later repealed December 1933.

SCANDAL

Believers will readily admit their religion in not a perfect institution and most forgive when a scandal becomes known. That said, such scandals shake a religious community, and followers may decide to abandon their faith.

Religious scandals may be isolated incidents perpetrated by individuals; however, others result from a systemic flaw or failure within the religious organization itself resulting in multiple offenses occurring over extended periods. The shame caused by these scandals, sometimes of a criminal nature, are more grievous especially if they are concealed or denied when confronted. Extensive sexual abuse cases by Catholic religious that have become known is a shameful example.

ZEALOTRY

Religious zealotry may or may not be sinister. A determined pursuit of one's religious convictions need not be scorned. Some believe the austerity of a Trappist monk residing in the Abbey of Gethsemane in Kentucky as zealotry. They may consider a life of silence, celibacy, obedience, and isolation within a cloister as earmarks of a zealot. If so, fine. No harm done. A monk's personal spiritual lifestyle decision is worthy of admiration and respect.

However, history is replete with incidences of harmful religious zealousness, particularly by the hands of governments and powerful religious interests. The Inquisitions, the Crusades, Jihads by the sword, cruel Sharia punishments, certain incidences of ethnic cleansings and apartheid justified on religious grounds are examples of zealousness trampling human decency.

AFTERWORD

The scholar Joseph Campbell wrote in *A Hero's Journey*, *"God is a metaphor for a mystery that absolutely transcends all human categories of thought, even the categories of being and non-being. Those are categories of thought. I mean it's as simple as that. So, it depends on how much you want to think about it. Whether it's doing you any good. Whether it is putting you in touch with the mystery that's the ground of your own being. If it isn't, well, it's a lie.*

So, half the people in the world are religious people who think that their metaphors are facts. Those are what we call theists. The other half are people who know that the metaphors are not facts. And so, they are lies. Those are the atheists."

Campbell sums it up for me. I am no longer a theist. I have found ultimate meaning in philosophy and psychology. These satisfy and provide grounding for the meaning of life, explaining human nature and espousing ethical principles for individuals, communities, and governments.

I do not consider the hereafter a relevant concern or a possibility. Prayer is wishful thinking and no substitute for action. Meditation drawn from spiritual traditions can be observed just as well without religious doctrine attached.

The two principal insights of religion are gratitude (worship) and acceptance (God's will). Every person is capable of appreciating and accepting without theological trappings. Our moral compass comes naturally when our parents do a responsible job of modeling and training good behavior. Charity begins at home where generosity is modeled, beginning with loving parents.

American writer Isaac Asimov (1920 – 1992) wrote:
"I have never, not for one moment, been tempted toward religion of any kind. The fact is that I feel no spiritual void. I have my philosophy of life, which does not include any aspect of the supernatural."

"I am an atheist, out and out. It took me a long time to say it. I've been an atheist for years and years, but somehow I felt it was intellectually unrespectable to say one was an atheist, because it assumed knowledge that one didn't have. Somehow it was better to say one was a humanist or an agnostic. I finally decided that I'm a creature of emotion as well as of reason. Emotionally I am an atheist. I don't have the evidence to prove that God doesn't exist, but I so strongly suspect he doesn't that I don't want to waste my time."

It is high time that atheism becomes respectable. The notion that it spawns immorality and criminality is ignorant. The "Golden Rule" is the universal ethical mandate for all to follow.

PERSPECTIVES

MY LIFE, TIMES & CONVICTIONS

CHAPTER IV

WHAT I LEARNED ABOUT LEADERSHIP

CONTENTS

Preface 80
Communicability 81
Approachability 82
Truthfulness 83
Integrity 84
Candor 85
Listening 86
Humility 87
Good-Humor 88
Equanimity 89
Patience 90
Compassion 91
Prudence 92
Delegation 93
Teamwork 94
Problem Solver 95
Decisiveness 96
Afterword 97

PREFACE

I had the privilege of serving in leadership capacities in U.S. hospitals and multi-hospital systems for thirty years. I was fortunate to become a hospital CEO at age 29 and so faced the challenges of senior leadership my entire career. Over that period, my leadership skills were tested, and through successes and failures learned about leadership. Now retired, I decided to share my hard-earned perspectives concerning leadership with aspiring executives.

I do not envy my colleagues in the field today who are leading healthcare entities during the devastating Covid-19 pandemic. They are facing unprecedented challenges I had never faced. These dire circumstances highlight how important sound leadership is for keeping an organization true to its mission and meeting the challenges that sometime are overwhelming.

A hospital is good place to learn and practice leadership due its scope and complexity. A hospital is a hotel, it is medical-surgical units, a laboratory, a 24-hour cafeteria, a radiation department, an intensive care unit, a chapel, a morgue, a gift shop, a training center, a supply depot, a helicopter pad, a boiler plant, an underground reservoir of oil for the emergency generators and more. In addition to its own staff and medical personnel, it also functions in partnership with an independent medical staff granted privileges to care for their patients. Together, this partnership serves the communities 24/7, 365 days a year. The leader usually reports to a Board of Trustees who expect superior performance in terms of quality, accreditation, meeting community needs and financial sustainability.

I attended the University of Michigan School Public Health in Ann Arbor, Michigan to earn an MPH in medical care organization. This important academic grounding was only the foundation. A leader must continue learning by self-refection, reading, conferences, and from association with colleagues.

The author I admire most and drew a great deal of inspiration and wisdom from is management guru, Peter Drucker. His maxim, "Management is doing things right; leadership is doing the right things" says so much.

If by sharing what I have learned about leadership using actual anecdotes from my own experience contributes to the reader's understanding, I will have accomplished my purpose.

COMMUNICABILITY

Whether someone is an extrovert or introvert, they still must communicate effectively. This may seem obvious, but it is essential to establish trust, set direction and priorities, seek understanding, dispel, and prevent misinformation, answer questions and welcome input. Hospitals -- like all human organizations -- are social creatures and communication is an artery that must flow continually.

ANECDOTE #1.

I have had to impose major layoffs two times in my career. If there was a time for effective communication, these were it. This required 'town-hall' type meetings to meet face-to-face, be transparent about the need, clear about the process, seek understanding and, very importantly, allow feedback.

In my first CEO position in a rural community hospital, I had a monthly 'call-in' radio program, and I wrote a weekly column in the local press. Sometimes these allowed me to announce new initiatives, introduce new medical staff, and at times diffuse irate caller's comment with facts and rationale. Whether in person or through public relations staff, external communications are vital too.

DISCUSSION

In his book *Managing the Non-Profit Organization*, Drucker stresses another essential aspect of communication: LISTENING. He says, "Listening is not a skill; it's a discipline. Anybody can do it. All you have to do is keep your mouth shut." Communication is a two-way street.

APPROACHABILITY

Approachability may seem an odd and insignificant topic; but I beg to differ. The leader must be approachable because his or her span of control covers the entire employee base. The leader commands the attention of everyone, so being approachable indicates a willingness to listen.

ANECDOTE #2.

After two years away, I returned for a brief visit to the hospital where I was the CEO for seven years. As I walked down the main corridor, a housekeeper approached, and our eyes met. She still recognized me. We stopped and greeted each other with smiles. Out of pure curiosity, I asked her how she like the present CEO. She said not so much. I was a bit shocked and expressed surprise and said, "can you tell me why"? She said, unlike you, every time he passes me in the corridor, he just ignores me.

DISCUSSION

Approachability presumes acknowledgement. Empathy and sound labor relations demand leaders show respect for employee whenever possible, whether housekeepers or department heads. Even a 'hi' or a smile in passing means you care, and they are an important part of the team. For that housekeeper this meant dignity and validation. Open-door policies, touring the halls and simply showing respect to ALL employees -- not just VIPs -- uplifts organizational morale.

TRUTHFULNESS

Americans have learned the devastation a *BIG LIE* can wreak. Leaders who promulgate them do so at their own peril.

ANECDOTE #3.

A month after I arrived as CEO, I received a letter from the National Labor Relations Board (NLRB) setting the date for a union vote. Service and technical employees had signed petitions. They wanted representation by the American Federation of State, County and Municipal Employees (AFSCME). My first thought was wondering if the former CEO left because this labor issue was brewing. This was a complete surprise. I am not anti-union if conditions warrant, but this would be the first union there and I did not want adversarial labor relationships. I retained a labor attorney who advised that I meet affected employees and ask them to reconsider. Over a couple weeks, I invited groups to 10 – 12 affected staff to the board room. I told them candidly that we could not afford any raises beyond normal cost of living adjustments (COLA); but, if financial conditions permitted, I would do my best to do more. I also stressed I wanted harmonious labor relations and I had an open-door policy and would do my best to support them any way I could. The unionization drive was defeated by comfortable margin.

DISCUSSION

Truthfulness builds trust and will likely get 'the benefit of the doubt'. I had no more labor union unrest during my tenure.

INTEGRITY

Integrity means having strong ethical moral principles both personally and in the conduct of business. Dwight Eisenhower remarked that the supreme quality for leadership is unquestionably integrity.

ANECDOTE #4.

When I became a Senior Vice President at a large multi-hospital system with over 100,000 employees that recently formed from a merger, the CEO added on additional role to my portfolio. He asked me to serve as Chief Responsibility Officer (CRO) reporting directly to the Board of Trustees. I was told I was given the position as I was considered a leader of utmost integrity. The role was established to create and lead a system-wide compliance program that would promote, detect and restore corporate integrity should it fail due to systemic or individual failures, intentional or not.

DISCUSSION

Reputation, the face of integrity, is vital for success whether personal or institutional. Nothing degrades reputation like scandal or any failure of integrity. This is especially true for the highly visible leader. A stellar reputation breeds respect and commitment. Lapses destroy morale and put the organization in peril. The classic case is Enron Corp. where the CEO's and CFO's deceptions led its bankruptcy and auditor, Arthur Andersen, lost its customers and ceased operating.

CANDOR

Candor promotes clarity and is a sign of sincerity. Sincere comes from the Latin and means "pure", not fake or watered down, especially when the message is a difficult one.

ANECDOTE #5.

A clear indication that our chief of medical staff was a misogynist surfaced in the hospital's public cafeteria while we were enjoying lunch with my director of nursing. This chief got very emotional, raised his voice, and began to "chew-out" Marge, the nursing director. The reason did not matter. I was incensed. She was totally embarrassed of course. I was always protective of my nursing staff, and this crossed the line.

I confronted him head-on. I told him calmly yet candidly to NEVER treat Marge or any other nurse that way again. He did not accept the message; however, the next day I got his formal letter saying I could no longer attend any medical staff meetings. I went to the next Board of Trustees meeting with a board resolution to amend the medical staff bylaws to make the CEO ex-officio at every medical staff meeting. That ended the crisis. That medical chief of staff and I got along well after that was settled.

DISCUSSION

Speaking truth to power is not easy. A good leader not only speaks with candor but expects it from everyone. This two-way dialogue is key to identifying opportunities as well as shortcomings. The leader must create an environment of candor.

LISTENING

While leaders like to hear themselves talk, the best prefer to listen. The latter is much more effective in keeping a finger on the pulse of the organization.

ANECDOTE #6.

I heard via the 'grape-vine' our most senior employee about to retire was terribly upset. I invited her into my office. She said she met the HR director to discuss her pension. He told her the HR records showed a remarkable tenure of 29 years. She became agitated saying it was 30 years. She was sure of it. This proud benchmark of 30 years meant so much to her. The director said sorry, the correct number was twenty-nine and her pension based on it.

She had left his office distraught and shared her disgust and disappointment with anyone who would listen. I excused myself and called the HR director. I asked him what the difference was in her pension of one year. He told me it was a few dollars. No surprise, as the plan was meager. I rejoined that dear lady and informed her I believed her and instructed the HR director to credit the 30 years. Delighted, she was able to enjoy her retirement party. This helped the morale in Housekeeping Dept.

DISCUSSION

Listening with empathy is a powerful attribute for a leader. Arrogance and hubris are deafening. Do not succumb. Considering these particular facts after listening, my decision was correct. The lovely lady was now eager to come back to visit on occasion.

HUMILITY

My favorite definition of humility is, "knowing your place and taking it." This means keeping your Ego in check. Leaders who get carried away with their Ego are headed for trouble.

ANECDOTE #7.

The only time I was demoted came late in my career. We had merged two health systems. I was an executive in one of these systems for ten years. I was given responsibility over Risk Management that included two insurance programs which had not yet been merged. The one from the other former system suffered a huge spike in claims reserves that created havoc. We had a leadership meeting, and I was asked why this had happened. I had examined this matter and gave my candid opinion.

A powerful executive from that other former system exploded, accused me of fabricating. It was a bold-face lie, she yelled. I learned a lesson in diplomacy. I must have overstated by case and come across as arrogant. The next day, the CEO took Risk Management from my portfolio. I humbly accepted expressing regret and declaring it was simply the truth as I saw it. Wanting to remain there and contribute, I ate 'humble pie". I still get upset thinking about that incident.

DISCUSSION

Swiss moral philosopher, Henri Frédéric Amiel (1821 – 1881) said, "There is no respect for others without humility in oneself." Whenever I saw executives who seemed too preoccupied with their stature, I cringed. Some were wily enough to succeed, but I would never want to work for this kind of leader.

GOOD-HUMOR

If I had started a hospital department head meeting with this quote from Will Roger, "always drink upstream from the herd," I bet this would have relaxed the team a bit and maybe usher in some creative thinking. Next to humility, being good humored is an enviable trait for a leader.

ANECDOTES #8.

This still makes me laugh. In around 1979, I was heading out for work one morning, about to get into my car. An unbelievably strong and pungent odor overwhelmed me. I instantly recognized what it was. A skunk must have unloaded *recently nearby although I did not notice one. I regained my bearing and drove off.*

At that time, our corporate office was in the motherhouse of the religious order who sponsored our health system. I settled into my office desk. About five minutes later, two nuns walked pass my door and down the corridor. About three seconds later I heard one say quite loudly, "Oh My What Stinks!" I suddenly realized I was the culprit. Oh my! Too embarrassed to admit it, I discreetly went home to change. I just chuckled.

DISCUSSION

Unlike Abe Lincoln who an expert storyteller, if you are like me and cannot crack a decent joke, I would still try to use humor to beneficial effect, beginning with a pleasant affect. Hospitals can be serious, stressful, and somber places. Humor is vitally important to refresh, relax and revive morale. Leaders need to join-in, not take themselves too seriously, smile and welcome humor wherever and whenever it is appropriate.

EQUANIMITY

Problems reaching the leaders attention are generally not trivial. Often a 'knee-jerk' reaction is not the best one. It requires equanimity: composure and thoughtful reflection.

ANECDOTES #9.

Looking back thirty years, the biggest crisis I faced was a medical staff revolt. Our pathologists had been with us for years. They were well established and highly regarded. The problem was Medicare dramatically cut reimbursement for pathology services. Our group covered rural hospitals; sort of a 'milk run' 3 days a week to do frozen sections, other pathology work and supervise the laboratory. I met with the lead pathologist to discuss a reduction in fees in line with the new reimbursement. He refused saying they would have to give in to all the area hospitals.

Another pathology group offered their services well within the new reimbursement regulations. I decided to make the change and informed the medical staff. A revolt erupted mainly by the surgeons. Rumors of my demise surfaced. I took time to think this though calmly. I decided to have an emergency meeting of the entire medical staff. I let the enraged doctors speak first. After sharing details of the excellent credentials of the new pathologists, I went to a white board and presented the financial situation in detail. Medical staff seemed surprised by the high fees we were paying presently. Influential medical staff members began to speak up supporting my decision. I finally got sleep.

DISCUSSION

Leaders need to practice equanimity to calmly assess matters and determine the most prudent action to take.

PATIENCE

We should never confuse patience with indecisiveness. Someone can exercise patience and be timely; it is not a delaying tactic. Patience is more akin to maturing, ripening, deliberative. Patience and perseverance correlate as well. Martin Luther King Jr. exemplifies a leader who had a supreme command of patience. A leader is well served if he holds a deep reserve of patience.

ANECDOTES #10.

Mergers are always challenging. This was my greatest test of patience. In 1999, after considerable deliberations, two health systems came together to form one of largest healthcare systems *in the USA and still is today. I was given the privilege and challenge of serving as Transition Project Manager for our system paired with my counterpart from the other system. We formed multiple committees to address governance, financial, human resources, cultural, and a host of operational issues.*

This work ran the gamut of renaming the merged entity to publishing new Mission and Vision statements, preparing legal documents, forming the new management team, and settling on what city the corporate headquarters would be domiciled. It required deliberation, preparation, travel, and patience. Two organizations exercised patience together until they achieved their goal and, post-merger, has been extraordinarily successful merger.

DISCUSSION

Patience will lubricate addressing huge challenge such as a corporate merger. *"If I had six hours to chop down a tree, I would spend the first four hours sharpening the axe,"* said Abraham Lincoln. Preparation and patience go together.

COMPASSION

From the Latin root words that means "to suffer together with", there is no more important attribute for a healthcare leader literally or figuratively. And it is well served for any corporate executive. Compassion led most medical, nursing, and other technical staff to enter the healing professions.

ANECDOTES #11.

My opportunities to show and observe compassion began in my first job in a hospital to earn a salary to get through college. I entered an orderly training program and became the night 'house orderly' in a 450-bed medical center. I was stationed in a base unit until my pager beeped me, then I moved through the 'house", floor to floor, unit to unit to do all the usual orderly tasks: male catheters, enemas, CPR during codes, stat EKGs, etc. I was often stationed in 1 West, the neuro unit that usually cared for comatose patients. I still recall how compassionate the nursing staff were with these comatose patients. The nurses were gentle and would even talk to these patients while cleaning them and giving them clean sheets. They treated them like family. The compassion was palpable and inspiring. As a CEO years later, I wanted the entire organization, including myself, to treat all patients, visitors, and each other with this degree of care, sensitivity, and empathy.

DISCUSSION

Compassion is not just a trait of good leadership; it is a human trait. However, it is essential when leading a service organization such as a hospital. A leader in any service organization will "set the tone" if he or she is perceived as a compassionate person.

PRUDENCE

In a February 2020 article in the *Harvard Business Review* entitled "Lead Your Business Through the Coronavirus Crisis" by Martin Reeves, Nikolaus Lang and Philipp Carlsson-Szlezak, the authors cite PRUDENCE as one of six characteristics necessary in a crisis policy response. Exercising judgement based on careful consideration of all the options is prudence at work.

ANECDOTES #12.

One of our finest surgeons came to my office, closed the door, and asked me to help him. He just discovered his patient had *a surgical sponge left in after a relatively minor surgery. But this required another corrective surgery. He did not want his reputation sullied by making this a public issue. He said he would tell the patient there was a complication that needed to be addressed without being overly explicit. He had a wonderful rapport with that patient and felt this would remain such he if could manage this with discretion with the hospitals help.*

Prudence is a moral virtue. I weighed the duty of full disclosure against the loyalty lost if I did not agree with the suggested course. Given these circumstances and the long-term repercussions I could envision, I agreed and waived the hospital fees and alerted key nurses of how we would proceed. I never second-guessed my decision. It was prudent. The patient left content after a few extra days and enjoyed a full recovery. 'Having the surgeon's back' paid huge dividends later.

DISCUSSION

Sometime the most delicate and tough decisions require a big dose of prudence especially if the circumstances are ambiguous or fraught with ethical dimensions.

DELEGATION

Three important reasons to delegate: (1) if the leader is weak in any area of competence, delegate this to someone competent; (2) delegating allows the leader to develop staff and this will highlight those who excel and are ripe for promotion; (3) a leader understands nothing hurts morale as badly as a 'micro-managing',

ANECDOTES #13.

My office had a large painting of a scene overlooking Jerusalem like the picture here. Every time I looked at it, I was reminded that my responsibility as leader was over the entire organization. To be effective, I had to address 'big picture' issues while confidently delegating day to day tasks to capable staff.

DISCUSSION

An effective delegator supports his direct reports in three ways: 1) makes clear how periodic reporting should occur. Some leaders prefer written reports; others verbal reports or a combination; 2) provide for their professional development; and 3) make sure they have the authority commensurate with the responsibilities assigned.

TEAMWORK

Healthcare operations, like large firms, is a team enterprise. Teams within and across the organization need to meld collective talents to accomplish important work. Building esprit décor is a vital element of superior performance. Leader must display team leadership skills and promote and encourage team effort throughout the organization.

ANECDOTES # 14.

In the winter of 1978, Michigan had a blizzard with massive amounts of snowfall. Our town near Lake Michigan was hit particularly hard with lake effect snow squalls. Transportation was paralyzed for several days until front-end loaders could clear the streets. Staffing was becoming a huge issue. As CEO, I knew I had to do whatever I could to relieve the stress and manage the situation until back to normal.

I spread the word we needed snowmobiles to get staff in. Employees' families with snowmobiles began to ferry staff. We were near completion of a major expansion project. I had areas cleaned and we placed mattresses and bedding throughout. Staff had a place to sleep after multiple shifts. We open the cafeteria 24/7 for everyone free of charge. My hospital career began as an orderly. I put on scrubs and performed orderly duties to assist the nurses. These efforts and others helped pull everyone together to make sure patients were cared for until the roads were cleared.

DISCUSSION

Famous coach Vince Lombardi said, *"I don't necessarily have to like my players and associates but as their leader I must love them. Love is loyalty, love is teamwork, love respects the dignity of the individual. This is the strength of any organization."*

PROBLEM SOLVER

Problem solving is a challenge for any organization. Former General Colin Powell remarked, *"The day soldiers stop bringing you their problems is the day you have stopped leading them. They have either lost confidence that you can help or concluded you do not care. Either case is a failure of leadership."*

ANECDOTE #15.

Back in 1978 there were no I-phones. The world's first cell phone was launched in 1983. It was the Motorola DynaTAC 800x. It was priced at around $4,000 and lasted for 30 minutes of talk time before dying. It was also about the size of a foot long sub from Subway. The medical staff at my hospital had to be tethered to landlines whenever 'on-call'. No hunting or fishing and even grocery shopping away from a telephone. I wanted their lives to be a more comfortable. It was not a severe problem, but I wanted a fix.

I contacted Motorola and got a quote on a freestanding radio antenna with sufficient area coverage. We installed it on hospital's roof, trained our operators and issued pagers. You can imagine the delight of medical staff who now could have more freedom of movement when not in the hospital.

DISCUSSION

Generally speaking, if an organization is overwhelmed with problems, this is a sign of poor leadership and management. I have had to let go managers who seems to have constant turmoil in their area of responsibility.

DECISIVENESS

Whether in problem solving, a major strategic matter, or managing a crisis, a leader must be decisive. Authority without execution is pointless. A leader's credibility degrades quickly if they cannot make decisions in a clear and timely manner.

ANECDOTE #16.

I became an interim CEO for a three-hospital system in the Southwest. I interviewed each Vice President privately to get acquainted, understand their scope of responsibility and status report on key issue they were addressing. I also asked about the effectiveness of the leadership as a team. Almost everyone singled out one fellow Vice President as being divisive, extremely difficult to work and not effective in her role. This matter had been lingering for years; the former CEO had hired this person and did not agree nor want to address the matter.

I decided to make my own independent assessment. After a month, I came to a similar conclusion; termination was warranted. I met with the person, discussed how I arrived at my decision and asked the party to work with HR on a severance package that we had preplanned. The leadership team rallied behind this decision. I did not leave this matter for the next CEO to deal with. It was the right thing to do.

DISCUSSION

Gestalt psychologist, Frits S. Perls (1893 – 1970), used to parse the word responsibility into 'response-ability' because he wanted the meaning to stress the 'ability to respond' and not on authority, obligation, or status. Decisiveness is responsibility in action. I agree with Fritz 100%.

AFTERWORD

What does a hospital and war have in common? Lives are at stake. One preserves; the other destroys. As dramatically opposite as their missions are, the leadership qualities required are similar just as they apply universally to all organizations. To evaluate the list of leadership attributes I found desirable, I have offer characteristics of two famous generals that I admire.

DWIGHT D. EISENHOWER (1890 – 1969)

In an address by John Addison on Aug 29, 2016, entitled *'Cultivating Leadership'*, he cited five leadership characteristics of Eisenhower:

BEING A LIKEABLE LEADER

Eisenhower loved and cared for his troops. He understood that when you go into a battle, it is your teamwork, your love for one another, that is going to pull you through.

"Morale is born of loyalty, patriotism, discipline, and efficiency, all of which breeds confidence in self and in comrades... Morale is at one and the same time the strongest and the most delicate of growths. It withstands shocks, even disasters of the

battlefield, but can be destroyed utterly by favoritism, neglect or injustice."

PRACTICING OPTIMISM

Eisenhower knew that to have positive, confident troops, he would have to lead by example.

"Optimism and pessimism are infectious, and they spread more rapidly from the head downward than in any other direction."

CONTROLLING YOUR EGO

Eisenhower managed the egos of others, pulling them together for a common cause. He was effective because he could subjugate his own ego, and he really saw himself as a normal GI.

"Always take your job seriously, but never yourself."

KNOWING YOUR PURPOSE

Eisenhower sold his people on the mission and got his men engaged in the larger cause—he was always able to make sure the team understood the "why" behind the "what.

"Soldiers, sailors and airmen of the Allied Expeditionary Forces, you're about to embark upon the great crusade toward which we have striven all these many months. The eyes of the world are upon you. The hopes and prayers of liberty-loving people everywhere march with you."

TAKING RESPONSIBILITY

Too often leaders want the credit, but when things do not go well, they do not want the blame. Eisenhower was different. Here was a man at the greatest moment of his life, who knew his attempts might not succeed, so he wrote a letter— "In Case of Failure"—because he was willing to take the blame.

"Our landings in the Cherbourg-Havre area have failed to gain a satisfactory foothold, and I have withdrawn the troops. My decision to attack at this time and place was based upon the best information available. The troops, the air, and the Navy did all that bravery and devotion to duty could do. If any blame or fault attaches to the attempt, it is mine alone."

ULYSSES S. GRANT (1822– 1885)

In his 2018 article, "Ulysses S. Grant: 12 Leadership Lessons", Sean P. Murray cites these attributes of Grant:

DECISIVENESS

Grant understood that making a wrong decision was bad, but often delaying the decision altogether was much worse. "In war anything is better than indecision," Grant said. "If I am wrong, we shall soon find out, and can do the other thing, but not to decide wastes both time and money and may ruin everything."

COOLNESS UNDER PRESSURE

When the heat of battle was on, Grant could remain calm, and his thinking remained lucid. Lincoln was frustrated by of his generals, but not Grant. Lincoln commented: "The great thing about Grant is his perfect coolness and consistency of purpose...he is not easily excited, and he has the grit of a bulldog."

NEVER BLAME OTHERS

If there was a mistake or things did not go well, Grant always took responsibility. In a famous dispatch to Lincoln during the war he wrote, "Should my success be less than I desire...the least I can say is, the fault is not with you."

INTEGRITY

Grant was raised in an abolitionist family. He always believed that slavery was a moral evil. Although Grant could have raised a considerable sum of money if he had sold a slave he was given, he promptly freed him. He never placed money or fame above his own integrity.

GIVE CREDIT AWAY

While composing a dispatch to President Lincoln, he wrote: "I propose to fight it out on this line if it takes me all summer." Then in a simple yet bold move he struck the word "me" from the message, and completely transformed it from a personal note to a powerful rallying cry. After all, he was not holding the line by himself. Grant understood that it was his men, the entire Army of the Potomac that was working together to hold their position. It became one of his most famous lines from the Civil War.

DON'T HIDE BEHIND UNIFORMS OR TITLES
JUST BE YOURSELF

He never relied on his rank or uniform to command the respect of others. He earned respect through his leadership.

LISTEN TO OTHERS AND BE RESPECTFUL

Grant was an expert listener and communicator. He would take the time to listen to his staff officers and soldiers. And when he was not listening, he would tell stories using humor. One of Grant's officers, Ely Parker.

PERSPECTIVES

MY LIFE, TIMES & CONVICTIONS

CHAPTER V

TITANS OF PERFORMANCE

FRIEDRICH S. PERLS M.D.

&

PETER F. DRUCKER

CONTENTS

Preface.. 105
Introductions... 107
On Mission... 108
On Leadership.. 108
On Environment... 110
On Ego.. 111
On Decisions.. 112
On Awareness.. 113
On Attitude.. 114
On Performance... 115
On Innovation.. 116
On Marketing... 117
On Strategy.. 119
On Teambuilding... 120
On Motivation.. 122
On Effectiveness.. 122
On Communications.. 123
Afterword... 125

PREFACE

Friedrich (Fritz) Salomon Perls and Peter Ferdinand Drucker are two of the most consequential original thinkers of the twentieth century.

Fritz Perls (1893 – 1970)　　**Peter Drucker (1909 – 2005)**

Fritz Perls, a German born American, is the originator of Gestalt Therapy. A psychiatrist and psychoanalyst trained in the Freudian school, he fled Nazi Germany and settled in Johannesburg, South Africa where he reassessed Freud's work. In his seminal first book, *"Ego, Hunger & Aggression"*(1947), he debunked much of Freudian theory replacing it with psychological insights grounded in phenomenology and existential philosophy. Much of his career was dedicated to perfecting his unique therapy techniques and training future therapists.

Peter Drucker, an Austrian born American, is regarded as the inventor of modern management. A prolific author, consultant and professor, his contributions to management theory and practice brought him international acclaim. His book, *"Concept of the Corporation"* (1946), a study of General Motors Corporation, launched his illustrious career in the USA. A prolific author, he was a highly sought-after consultant and lecturer throughout his life. He may be the most admired management thinker of our time.

In pursuit of a Master of Arts (MA) degree in *Counseling & Personnel* at Western Michigan University followed by a Master of Public Health degree (MPH) in *Healthcare Management* at the University of Michigan, I gained a keen appreciation for both thinkers and drew on their wisdom often in my personal life and thirty-year career as a hospital CEO and health system executive. Perls and Drucker share these characteristics:

- Each intensely disdained Nazi Germany. Perls, a Jew, fled Germany for South Africa. Drucker immigrated to England. He wrote on the dangers of *Fascism* in his first book, *"The End of Economic Man"* in 1939.
- Each were influenced by Danish philosopher/theologian Søren Kierkegaard and existentialism.
- Each were extremely keen observers of people and process, gifted writers, and teachers.
- Each produced original seminal works of theories and practices.
- Each focused principally on people: Perls as a physician and psychotherapist; Drucker as a social scientist.
- Each appreciated and keenly understood and pursued the notion of 'performance'. Drucker on managerial and organizational performance; Perls on personal performance, aka human potential.

Given these similarities, Drucker and Perls might have been contemporary 'kindred spirits'. Sadly, I found no indication they met or collaborated. I could only imagine the kind of dialogue these two *"Titans of Performance"* might have exchanged. I have attempted this here using a *Socratic-like* dialogue. This represents a tiny sampling of their thinking. My objectives are twofold: to highlight how their thinking parallel in many respects and stimulate the readers' interest in exploring their works further and applying their wisdom for their own personal and professional growth

INTRODUCTIONS

PETER: *I am so pleased to meet you. May I call you Fritz?*

FRITZ: *Sure, and I assume Peter is ok with you?*

PETER: *Absolutely. I understand you came to Big Sur in 1963. I joined the faculty in Claremont Graduate Univ. in 1973. Surely, our paths have crossed; sorry we have not met before now.*

FRITZ: *I agree. Let us make the most of today then. I suppose we will be speaking English, although we may be tempted to slip into our native Deutsch. (Fritz grins).*

PETER: *I suppose our readers would not appreciate that. Since we have been Americans most of our lives, English is better anyway, don't you think? (Peter smiles).*

FRITZ: *Yes! As we have already agreed on a number of subjects of mutual interest to discuss, shall we begin?*

PETER: *Yes, Fritz, I will begin.*

ON MISSION

PETER: *I have said a thoughtfully constructed mission statement should be concise, such that you can put in on a T-shirt. It must reflect opportunity, commitment, and competence. The challenge then is for leadership to communicate the mission, so everyone understands it, embraces it, and abides by it. Results must evidence achievement of the mission.*

FRITZ: *While corporations have any number of mission statements, the individual -- in terms of psychology -- has one primary mission: self-actualization, to become a healthy, mature, functioning personality. I call this the fixed "end-gain" of a successful life, and I distinguishes this from the "means-whereby"; how each of us freely chooses our path to fulfill our destiny. Sometimes this clarity is helpful to a client.*

PETER: *I emphasize that an organization's mission must serve not only their internal stakeholders but the community and society at large. Social responsibility is not gratuitous, it is one key to sustainability.*

FRITZ: *You will see most of my remarks deal with the personality and not society. Nevertheless, although 'egoism' concerns self-interest, 'altruism' concerns the interests of others. A healthy personality needs to balance these two interests.*

ON LEADERSHIP

PETER: *I define leadership this way: leadership is the lifting of a man's vision to higher sights, the raising of a man's performance to a higher standard, the building of a man's personality beyond its normal limitations.*

FRITZ: *Peter, your definition works well for therapists. Each can positively impact the personal growth and potential of the individual. One serves the person; the other serves the organization. As a person matures as an individual, their capacity for leadership will likely increase as well.*

PETER: *The primary responsibility of the leader is directing the organization to do the 'right things' to achieve its mission. The task of the leader includes building an organizational structure and management team capable of doing things right so there is alignment of ends with means, effectiveness, and efficiency.*

FRITZ: *Peter, you also said, "there is nothing worse than doing the wrong thing well." This neatly describes a neurotic also. Compulsive disorders like alcoholism come to mind. For an organization, this behavior would be catastrophic. This certainly emphasizes the critical role of leaders in setting the proper course.*

PETER: *A successful leader must have humility and a willingness to delegate and listen. Arrogant leaders display the opposite, hubris. They fixate on past convictions, resist input, push results no longer relevant. They abuse their responsibility.*

FRITZ: *I prefer to parse the term, "response-ability" to emphasize taking effective action rather than having authority or obligation. The leader you describe as effective is less concerned with their own status and more concerned with performance.*

ON ENVIRONMENT

PETER: *From an organization's viewpoint, I consider the environment in several contexts:*

- *First, the ecological aspect. Organizations must assume and take responsibility for effective stewardship of the environments they impact. Safety and ergonomics within the footprint of the organization and preventing or mitigating pollution into the outside environment.*

- *Secondly, knowing one's customers and non-customers are vital to measuring results and searching for opportunities. This is accomplished by continual engagement with the outside environment.*

- *Thirdly, I mentioned social responsibility; that is committing the organization to making contributions for the greater good of their community and society.*

FRITZ: *Environment is extremely important in Gestalt work. Biologically, beginning with breathing, we live in a permanent cycle of interdependency with the environment. Psychologically, healthy individuals are in touch with two realities: themselves -- self-awareness -- and their environment. A neurotic or psychotic person has lost touch with one or both realities and is stuck living in a "fantasy" zone that I will discuss later.*

ON EGO

FRITZ: *The Ego is the functioning servant and executive of the personality. It is where awareness of reality and 'response-ability' is exercised. Freud identified three components of the personality: the Super-Ego (conscience), Id (urges), and Ego-Ideal (ideals, such as love). Unfortunately, his work focused only on Id (libido or sex instinct) and did not fully explain Ego function. I set forth my theories in my first book, "Ego, Hunger and Aggression" in 1947.*

Given any situation, the Ego experiences one or more of these influences (e.g., Super-Ego, Id or Ego-ideal), and sometimes all three simultaneously. These compete for the attention of the person and a healthy Ego identifies preferences and decides. This process operates at the boundary between us and the environment that we call 'Ego-boundary'. We call it the 'identification/alienation function'. I mention this as it has applicability in terms of the organization.

A child 'identifies' or bonds with its mother by extending its Ego-boundary to include mother. When members of a team identify with each other, they extend their Ego-boundaries to achieve team cohesion and their efforts are directed against an opposing (alien) team outside this boundary -- the competition.

PETER: *Fritz, you neatly describe the process of Ego-functioning. Ego also means* a person's sense of self-esteem or self-importance and at times 'over-importance'. *I have used the phrase 'investments in managerial Ego' or IMO to describe unproductive decisions about resource allocations that are Ego-based, rather than on results and opportunities. Your concept of Ego functions* *offers another extremely helpful idea. It considers opposing or conflicting viewpoints, that you call experiences.*

ON DECISIONS

PETER: *Effective decisions require a disciplined process. First, informed opinions need to be heard and debated necessary to determine what I call the "criterion of relevance" with the appropriate measurements. Then the facts and circumstances need to be examined and discussed considering the criterion. And the decision must lead to productive action to be relevant.*

I have also said the first step in a growth policy is not to decide where and how to grow. It is to decide what to abandon. To grow, a business must have a systematic policy to get rid of the outgrown, the obsolete, the unproductive.

FRITZ: *In Gestalt, the decision-process is part of the cycle of mental, sensory, and motor excitement and closure: the Ego function. When a person is 'centered' in the 'here and now', aware of its wants or needs, and of the situation or circumstances in their environment -- we call this 'figure-ground' awareness, effective decisions can be made. Let me cite two examples.*

Biologically, a hunger sensation creates excitement that provokes the decision to eat, to mobilize to find food – from the environment. Our balance is restored. Psychologically, if someone insults us, a sense of rage excites us. We can react and express anger or decide to ignore it. Both can bring closure and balance. However, letting the rage build into resentment creates an impasse, a lack of closure. Neurotics and psychotics lack the ability to achieve closure and balance.

ON AWARENESS

PETER: Awareness, particularly self-reflection is essential for professional development. I stated it succinctly in my book, "Managing Oneself". Knowledge workers must, effectively, be their own chief executive officers. It is up to you to carve out your place, to know when to change course, and to keep yourself engaged and productive during a work life that may span 50 years. To do those things well, you will need to cultivate a deep understanding of yourself – not only what your strengths and weaknesses are but also how you learn, how you work with others, what your values are, and where you can make the greatest contribution. Because only when you operate from strengths can you achieve true excellence.

FRITZ: I totally agree Peter. Awareness is at the heart of Gestalt therapy. Everything is grounded in awareness. Awareness is the only basis for knowledge, communication, growth, and the prerequisite of performance. Phobias and avoidances are neurotic conditions aimed at keeping awareness at bay, typically because it is unpleasant or an unfinished situation we do not want to confront, overcome, and get seek closure.

Leaders, like individuals, must contend with a culture of selfies and instant-happiness, instant-health, instant-cures. But that's not growth. That is all-surface stuff that distracts us from what is really happening within, our self-awareness. It also impedes our ability to suffer through pain which is essential for growth in certain situations like grief. While Gestalt is an encounter therapy to catalyze growth much quicker than psychoanalysis, it is not a quick fix. Maturation is a lifelong, step by step process.

Since awareness is so important, I would like to mention that one of Freud's great discoveries was a third zone of awareness. This is like a 'DMZ', a 'no-man's land' between awareness of self and the world. This mental zone has our fantasies, rehearsing, prejudices, opinions, artistic impulses. Healthy persons move between all three layers of awareness naturally.

A neurotic person spends too much time and energy in the DMZ. Psychotics and schizophrenics are out of touch with themselves or their world, or both, languishing in their DMZ fantasy layer. For example, a prejudice is a fixed idea in the DMZ, not open to reexamination. Resisting a Covid-19 vaccine after seeing a loved infected and perhaps passing away is a prime example of someone stuck in their prejudice fantasy DMZ.

For organizations, this DMZ layer may account for 'blind spots', biases, faulty thinking about the environment, looking inward and not outward. The interesting thing is that this zone is also an area of creativity when integrated properly with reality. Peter, you have described this as 'situational awareness' where the organization looks for creative solutions. I like your quote, "I don't predict, I just look out the window and see what's visible but not yet seen."

ON ATTITUDE

PETER: The most important question a worker can ask is, "what can I contribute?". This suggests an attitude vital for worker productivity throughout the organization. What I call "managerial attitude" is the worker's ability to see their worker as their supervisor does.

FRITZ: Attitude is vital for self-actualization. I have written, "So if you find out how you prevent yourself from growing, from using your potential, you have a way of increasing this, making life richer, making you more and more capable of mobilizing yourself. And your potential is based upon a very peculiar attitude: to live and review every fresh second."

ON PERFORMANCE

PETER: My career has been devoted primarily to thinking, writing, and consulting on performance of leaders and managers. The disciplines of management practice and its principles I have conceived are directed at making the organization perform. When there is alignment between the mission, management objectives and management practices, this drives results, the ultimate test of performance.

Another essential ingredient of a performing organization today is the knowledge worker, the most valuable asset of a 21st century organization because of their elevated levels of productivity and creativity. To stress this conviction, I have been a strong advocate for resisting 'outsourcing' which is a growing trend. This will have a detrimental effect on performance as it reduces the organization's commitment and ability to invest in, train and develop their own knowledge workers.

FRITZ: *Observe the biological roots of the words 'organization', 'corporation' or 'juridic person'. Gestalt psychology asserts the importance of the concept of 'holism', the unity of body and mind. This unity is vital aspect of performance.*

I consider performance in two ways: one relates to the human condition; the other in developing therapeutic skills. My career has been about assisting clients to perform better as human beings which mean maturing, overcoming neurotic behavior and dysfunctional thinking. We achieve this when clients discover, learn, and adopt more productive life-skills. This may sound cold, but humans waste a great deal of their potential. Our techniques are geared to boost their performance, to fulfill their destiny.

The other way I see performance is improving therapy skills. I tell aspiring therapists that I bring five things to the therapy session: my skills, two chairs for the client – one is the 'hot seat' to role play -- some tissue in case its needed, and my cigarettes. (Author's note: Perls was a chain smoker). I train future Gestalt therapy professionals on my theories and techniques to improve their performance on behalf of their clients.

PETER: *I have said, 'If you can't measure it, you can't manage it.' You cannot gauge performance without it. Measurement must be integrated into systems where processes, environmental factors and other results needs to be monitored and managed.*

ON INNOVATION

PETER: *In my book, "Innovation and Entrepreneurship", I proposed that Innovation be the central focus of the enterprise. I* *offered a theoretical framework to approach this systematically that includes these areas of focus:*

- *Unexpected occurrences.*
- *Incongruities.*
- *Process needs.*
- *Demographic changes.*
- *Changes in perception.*
- *New Knowledge*

FRITZ: *For mature persons, innovation mean self-actualization. When a leader or worker self-actualizes within the scope of their employment, they, and their organization benefits.*

Innovation relies on creative concentration, the convergence of attention and awareness in the here and now. We understand this in the phenomenon of 'serendipity', an unexpected or unintended discovery. This could easily be missed if someone is not paying very close attention to the structure and function under examination.

My definition of learning is 'discovery', that something is possible. A "learning organization" will stimulate innovation by expanding the creative impulses of its knowledge workers.

ON MARKETING

PETER: *Enterprises have two basic functions: innovation and marketing. All the rest are costs. Evaluating the external environment is essential. Knowing what the customer wants and values and satisfying it keeps the business relevant and sustainable. To market correctly is to "tune-in' to trends, the* *competition, non-customers, and new opportunities that feed into the strategic planning process. Marketing is not a function per se, but the whole business seen from the customer's point of view. Marketing cannot be not limited to the marketing department. Any knowledge worker can observe and contribute marketing insights if the organization welcomes this input.*

FRITZ: *Peter, Gestalt psychology has two principles that support your thinking regarding marketing. One we call the 'figure-ground' phenomenon illustrated by the graphic above. Depending on which figure (white or black) you focus on, that part will emerge. Go back & forth and you will see two pictures, two Gestalts. This principle suggests that an organization needs to understand both the figure and ground, the ground being the environment from which the figure emerges to get the fullest picture of what is there, what is happening now.*

Another concept is referred to as the "contact boundary". We use it to describe a person's Ego function that can distinguish between self-awareness and the environment. Healthy individuals naturally flow between self-awareness and awareness of the environment. Likewise, marketing suggests a constant flow of intelligence between what the organization is doing internally and how receptive or critical are its customers.

ON STRATEGY

PETER: *These are the key questions and issues in strategy development:*

- *What opportunities to pursue given attending risks.*
- *Concerns about scale, scope, and structure.*
- *Decisions about means: "make vs. buy".*
- *Compatibility of strategy with economic realities.*
- *Determine action steps to achieve objectives.*

Management's tasks are to strengthen what is producing results, remediate and improve what is desirable yet wanting, and eliminating the unnecessary. Opportunities, in part, come from shrewd and timely marketing. I have said, "the greatest danger in times of turbulence is not the turbulence; it is to act with yesterday's logic." Marketing is a compass to keep the organization heading true North.

FRITZ: *We teach clients to differentiate 'end-gain' which is determined by needs -- which is the primary thing -- and the 'means-whereby' to satisfy those need. In this way, we encourage them to take control of their lives for they have the freedom to choose how to satisfy their needs. This is strategic thinking of sorts. Applied to organizations, 'end-gain' would equate to strategic objectives and the "mean-whereby" to tactics, both essential for achieving results.*

ON TEAMBUILDING

PETER: *To achieve results, managers must harness commitment of staff, particularly if the strategy moves the organization in new directions beyond the status quo and out of the enterprises' 'comfort zone'. The leader of the past knew how to tell – the leader of the future will know how to ask. This cannot be achieved without collaboration, another word for teamwork. And you cannot produce results with a team without effective communications. Leaders that value and enable teamwork will have a "we" mindset and use that term rather an "I" and share the credit when the work is effective.*

One area where teambuilding is important is in the conduct of meetings. While I have said meetings are a symptom of bad organization, they are part of organizational life. The challenge is to keep them at a minimum and as productive as possible. So, they must be purposeful, properly prepared and facilitated. When meetings focus on solving problem and not identify opportunities, it is not paying attention on what matters most. Of course, problems must be paid attention to, but I often say if they are the only thing that is being discussed, opportunities will die of neglect.

FRITZ: *Gestalt psychology is now paying attention to group dynamics and the role of the team leaders. This includes keeping the team properly focused (the Gestalt principle of staying in the "here and now"); encouraging and celebrating "closure" when the team completes segments of work; keeping boundaries between team members respected; and "systems thinking" similar to what I mentioned before about sensory-motor functions.*

The following graphic was inspired by work at the Gestalt Institute of Cleveland. This depicts the dynamic cycle I have mentioned in personal terms, now expanded to organizational work. The rhythm of life is a series of unending Gestalts or closures seeking balance. Awareness combined with mindfulness (attention) are at the core of a maturing person or organization.

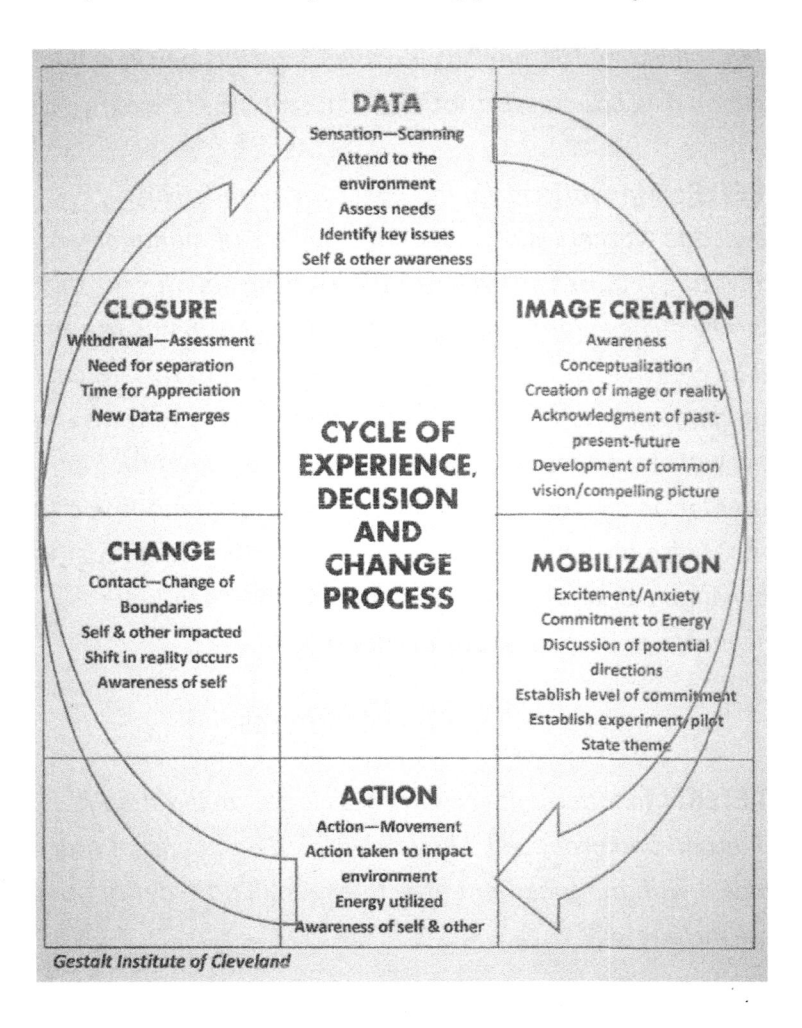

CYCLE OF EXPERIENCE, DECISION AND CHANGE PROCESS

DATA
- Sensation—Scanning
- Attend to the environment
- Assess needs
- Identify key issues
- Self & other awareness

IMAGE CREATION
- Awareness
- Conceptualization
- Creation of image or reality
- Acknowledgment of past-present-future
- Development of common vision/compelling picture

MOBILIZATION
- Excitement/Anxiety
- Commitment to Energy
- Discussion of potential directions
- Establish level of commitment
- Establish experiment/pilot
- State theme

ACTION
- Action—Movement
- Action taken to impact environment
- Energy utilized
- Awareness of self & other

CHANGE
- Contact—Change of Boundaries
- Self & other impacted
- Shift in reality occurs
- Awareness of self

CLOSURE
- Withdrawal—Assessment
- Need for separation
- Time for Appreciation
- New Data Emerges

Gestalt Institute of Cleveland

ON MOTIVATION

FRITZ: *The goal of therapy is to motivate people to take greater responsibility over their lives by helping them recognize self-defeating behaviors and psychological impediments that prevent personal growth. We then challenge and teach them how to overcome these barriers to growth. Gestalt therapy has been called "blitzkrieg therapy" as it achieves results quicker than Freudian psychoanalysis that could last months or even years.*

PETER: *Motivation that increases the productivity of knowledge workers is an essential objective of management. Motivating requires much more than raising salaries for this type of worker. They want engagement and opportunities to contribute and be creative. Delegation is one vital aspect of this. Micro-managing kills motivation. Effective Information systems that allow workers to see results in real time and allows for input to address problems or offer creative ideas and solutions in a timely manner also motivates and encourages performance. Lastly, knowledge workers want to understand how their work contributes to the entire organization.*

ON EFFECTIVENESS

PETER: *Management effectiveness is not an innate gift; it can be learned and practiced. I have identified a number of practices involved with management effectiveness. In no order of priority, these include:*

- *time management skills*
- *setting objectives and timelines*

- *organizing and prioritizing work*
- *prudent labor selections and relationships*
- *measuring progress and processes*
- *training & development*
- *thoughtful promotion and succession planning.*

Executives and workers need to be life-long learners in increase effectiveness. I also emphasize self-assessments and properly constructed employee appraisal systems to identify and improve strengths, avoid weak areas, and discover unique contributions.

FRITZ: *Managing the organization is no different than managing ourselves. Both require knowing what to prioritize. So, Peter, I resonate with your list. Another valuable attribute of a healthy person and effective manager is 'intuition' which is the intelligence of the organism. I have said that intelligence is the whole and intellect is the whore of intelligence. I coined the term "lose your mind and come to your senses." By putting all our energy in thinking and not seeing and hearing what is going on, you become handicapped and impede effectiveness.*

ON COMMUNICATIONS

FRITZ: *Communications starts with the 'I and You' and then transitions into the 'We' when true dialogue begins. Dialogue requires a 'sender' and a 'receiver'. Unfortunately, it is rare that people can 'talk' and 'listen'. Yet, this is essential for contact and understanding. In therapy, nonverbal communication, however, provides more information about the real essence of the person; this requires paying close attention to the client's body language such posture, movements, gestures, voice, and hesitations.*

Another aspect of communication that may be useful to the manager, as it does for the therapists, concerns asking the right questions. I instruct my therapists to focus on two essential questions, "what?" and "how?", not "why?". Let me explain. "What?" puts the matter in the here and now, centers on awareness and describes 'what is' being felt, thought, or dreamt. "How?" allows you to examine structure, see what is happening now and gain a deeper understanding of process. It provides perspective and orientation. These two questions are most productive for results in therapy. These two questions are a dramatic departure from Freud who kept asking "Why?", the foundation of psychoanalysis and most unproductive. It drums up rationalizations, excuses, avoidance, transference, attention on the past and not the present unfinished situation that the client needs to deal with.

"Why?" and "Because" are dirty word in Gestalt Therapy. One reason I pay as attention to affect, and non-verbal cues is my inherent distrust of language. I distinguish three classes of verbiage production: 'chickenshit' -- this is 'good morning', 'how are you'; 'bullshit'-- this is 'because', 'rationalization' and 'excuses'; and 'elephantshit' – when you talk about philosophy, existential Gestalt Therapy, etc. "Why?" gives only unending inquiries into the cause of the cause of the cause."

PETER: *Fritz, I also have said "the most important thing in communication is to hear what isn't being said." Yet, when communication is productive, as you stated, there is a connection between sender and receiver that generates understanding. I also say communication always makes demands. It always demands* *that the recipient become somebody, do something, believe something. It always appeals to motivation."*

FRITZ: *Peter, interesting. I believe the imperative, the demand, is the most effective form of communication. We agree.*

AFTERWORD

Perls and Drucker worked in two distinct fields – psychiatry and management consulting – yet their thinking seemed parallel in uncanny ways. A good example is a famous Drucker quote on communication, *"The most important thing in communication is hearing what isn't said."* This is incredibly close to what Perls wrote in *"Gestalt Therapy Verbatim"*: *"Verbal communication is usually a lie. The real communication is beyond words."*

Both were tenacious about getting results and they achieved it for themselves and others though their writing and mentoring. Their similarity may be due to their grounding and appreciation for existential philosophy. Their common abhorrence of fascism undoubtedly deepened their empathy for the human condition.

Perls exposed fundamental fallacies in Freudian psychoanalysis and totally rejected Freud's methods of therapy which could put clients on a couch for months or years with little progress. Yet, he gave Freud credit where due and went far beyond with original contributions inspired by phenomenology and Gestalt psychology. His therapy techniques were so powerful they have been described as "blitzkrieg" therapy; a rather ironic compliment given he fled Nazi Germany. Three attributes of his therapy account for its effectiveness. It requires face to face encounters between therapist and client. (Freud put clients on a couch not facing him). It was confrontational by insisting clients become aware of and face the unfinished business that brought them there. This requires an ability to recognize a client's tendency to avoid sensitive matters, and to skillfully bring them to a place where they can face and muster their own resources to work through the immediate problem.

Drucker is widely recognized as the father of modern management. He was an internationally recognized and sought-after consultant. Fortunately, he was blessed with longevity extending his prolific authorship to thirty-nine published books. He applied his uncanny ability to find the crux of matters in all areas of organizational life whether for-profit or non-profit corporations or government bureaucracies, attesting to his ability to nuance the unique challenges within each kind of organization faces. And then, when consulting in a particular organization, he could diagnose and prescribe a cogent set of recommendations.

Perls died in 1970 at age 76 when Drucker was 36 years of age. Drucker passed away in 2005 eight days before his 96th birthday. In terms of legacy, Drucker is well established as a management guru and will live on through his writings. Perls, to my regret, is not a household name like Freud or BF Skinner, the well know behavioral psychologist. My view is Perl's contributions were far more insightful about human psychology and how best to treat someone with mental affliction. Perls deserves to be elevated in stature. My hope is this work will in a modest way encourage this.

My respect for Drucker and Perls is immense. Neither Drucker nor Perls enjoy the same name recognition as their German-born contemporary, Albert Einstein, achieved, yet they were clearly trailblazers in their areas of expertise just as Einstein was in physics. Their contributions deserve wider study, recognition, and adoption. Each has earned recognition deserving the title, *"Titans of Performance"*.

PERSPECTIVES

MY LIFE, TIMES & CONVICTIONS

CHAPTER VI

ACHIEVING COPORATE COMPLIANCE EXCELLENCE
Step by Step Guide to Best Practice

CONTENTS

Preface.. 130
Governance... 132
Management... 133
CRO Appointment... 133
Culture & Compliance... 134
Program Funding.. 134
Program Organization.. 135
Program Name.. 137
Standards & Codes of Conduct............................ 138
Statutes & Regulations... 143
Program Publication... 144
Program Launch... 144
Periodic Compliance Training.............................. 145
Compliance Operations.. 146
Non-retaliation Policy.. 146
Occurrence Reporting.. 147
Hot-line Reporting... 148
Investigation.. 149
Remediation... 149
Case Management.. 150
Pfizer Compliance Program.................................. 151
Discussion.. 151

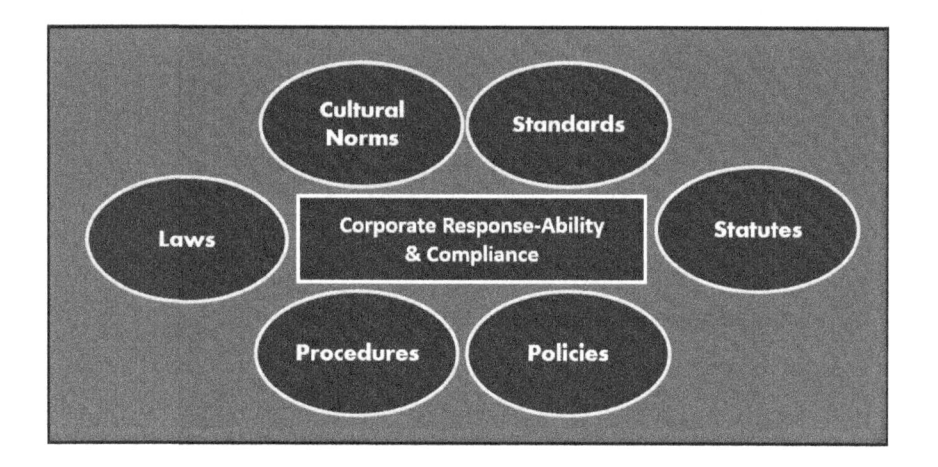

[Diagram: Central oval "Corporate Response-Ability & Compliance" surrounded by ovals labeled "Cultural Norms", "Standards", "Laws", "Statutes", "Procedures", "Policies"]

PREFACE

In 1999, two orders of Catholic religious sisters, the Daughters of Charity and the Sisters of St. Joseph of Nazareth, embarked on a process of discernment, negotiations and commissioning of multiple task force seeking operational recommendations. This culminated in agreement to merge their healthcare organization to create a new entity that became one of the largest Catholic sponsored healthcare systems in the United States. Initially, this new healthcare system comprised sixty-five hospitals -- and their related organizations -- in twenty-five states with over 100,000 employees (hereinafter called 'associates'). This system has grown considerably since its establishment. The parent company originally named *Ascension Health* later became *Ascension*: https://www.ascension.org/

Prior to the merger, I served as a senior vice president in one of the former systems; after merger, I retained the same title and was offered a new portfolio of responsibilities at the new corporate headquarters in St. Louis, Mo. I also accepted the position of *Corporate Responsibility Officer* (hereinafter 'CRO'). Some organizations call this a 'corporate compliance officer'.

The new board of trustees -- comprised of religious and lay persons -- and its newly appointed CEO and executive team recognized the importance of a CRP and gave it priority. It was abundantly clear from the beginning that proper conduct and monitoring compliance would a vital aspect of operations.

The wisdom and justification for having a CRP was made clear two years later when *Enron Corporation*, the Houston based energy & commodities firm with filed for bankruptcy in December 2001. This was followed by the dissolution of its external auditor, Arthur Andersen, one of the *Big Five* in the world at that time. Enron became the *'poster child'* for corrupt governance. Ironically, they did espouse core values but only on paper; they did not 'walk the talk'.

Scandals like those at *Enron* and *WorldCom* triggered the federal *Sarbanes-Oxley Act* of 2002 which enacted sweeping governance changes requiring companies to invest more in compliance. Whether voluntary and by external pressure, CRP constitutes a vital component of risk management for any organization intent on keeping its reputation and corporate integrity intact.

This manuscript is intended for organization evaluating a new CRP or for others to compare this CRP to theirs in the interest of possible improvements. Organized in a *step-by-step* process, it addresses essential rationale and features of our CRP that I had the privilege to help design, launch and oversee for ten years until my retirement. Though this CRP was designed for a large healthcare organization with multiple subsidiaries, the principles described herein are easily adapted into any organization whether a service or other type of enterprise.

GOVERNANCE

Trustees, directors or owners and officers of any corporation have legal duties of care, loyalty, and good faith. CRP is a vital instrument of governance for asserting and ensuring they fulfill these essential duties. CRP is built first to prevent non-compliant behaviors. However, should an untoward event arise out of malfeasance or unintentional, an effective CRP will serve to detect it, examine it, resolve, and remediate it. This is evidence of corporate good faith and commitment to good governance.

While governing boards entrust and delegate exercise of their fiduciary duties with an appointed chief executive officer (CEO), an important aspect of a well-designed CRP is it must encompass the entire organization, including the executive management team. As such, CRP requires independence and direct reporting to the governing board. Without continuous active commitment and oversight and involvement by the governing board, a CRP will not provide the necessary and sufficient level of oversight it was intended to afford.

MANAGEMENT

The CEO must be equally committed to CRP, or it will not be taken seriously within the organization and may be dismissed or rendered powerless in the face of misconduct. Obviously, any executive perpetrating misconduct will try to disable CRP and circumvent its intended purpose. When properly understood, valued, and operated, CRP becomes one of the organization's prime risk management mechanisms. Consequently, it also requires management's full commitment and attention with sound leadership and appropriate funding.

CRO APPOINTMENT

The CRO should be a member of the senior leadership team at the parent level and in all subsidiaries. The role needs this level of corporate visibility and authority. However, the CRO position may not need to be a full-time position particularly at the parent company level. Exposure is diffused throughout the entire organization. At the subsidiary level -- Ascension called these 'health ministries' -- the CRO may be full-time or part-time depending on the size and structure. With adequate staffing, the CRP can serve as a figurehead and delegate most functions to qualified staff.

The CRO at any level must first be a person of integrity with a firm commitment to the position. Having diplomacy, discretion, sound judgement and critical thinking skills are also vital attributes of an effective CRO. The CRP will uncover extremely sensitive and vexing problems. The CRO also needs administrative competence to ensure that the CRP functions are performed expertly and achieve intended results.

CULTURE & COMPLIANCE

There is a vital connection between the corporate culture and the CRP. They must be compatible and consistent. A sad yet poignant reminder is the dramatic and swift downfall of the governor of New York in 2021. Allegations surfaced by multiple women that described severe, pervasive, and unwelcome culture of sexual harassment. Although denied strenuously, there seemed to be enough evidence to suggest these allegations had merit.

As in the case of Enron and WorldCom, cultural gets set and modeled in executive offices by example. If CRP is merely a smokescreen and weakened by lack of attention or enforcement, it will become a drag on morale and accomplish nothing. At its best, a CRP will promote and enforce cultural norms that permeate the organization and serve as a systemic 'guard rail' to keep cultural integrity intact.

PROGRAM FUNDING

A well-designed CRP can be designed, staffed, and funded for a relatively modest sum for these reasons:

1. Most CRP operational requirements can be performed in the scope of management's normal responsibilities. This includes detection, reporting and remediation on CRP incidences.

2. Fortunately, in well-managed organization, the number of significant incidences requiring the involvement of CRP will be infrequent.

3. Due to this infrequency, the role of CRO and time and attention they must devote can, in most cases, be performed on a part-time basis or delegated to staff. In my case, the role of CRO took no more than 20% of my executive time and attention.

4. If full-time staff is required, this should be minimal. In our case, two full-time equivalents at the corporate level were needed. One was a professional CPA with interest in compliance and one clerical staff.

For these reasons, there is little economic justification for eschewing adoption of a CRP. The cost-benefit ratio is significant in favor of implementing this type of risk management program.

PROGRAM ORGANIZATION

In large corporations with subsidiaries that also have local governing boards, the reporting should be replicated at each level. In our case, each heath ministry appointed a CRO with dual reporting relationships to its own governing board and to me as CRO at the parent corporation, on a 'dotted-line basis'. If a subsidiary has no governing body, the CRO would report to their CEO and to me.

If there is discussion that the CRP program report to corporate legal counsel and operate under its direct purview, I advise against this, and this was not the case during my tenure. This structure creates a potential conflict of interest in my considered opinion. Corporate legal counsel is primarily responsible to protect or mitigate harm to the corporation per se. To avoid any tendency or temptation for legal counsel to subvert the full impact of CRP, CRP must function independently. An example of a potential conflict is a "whistleblower" which is encouraged in a well-operated CRP but may be considered a threat and impeded by legal counsel.

Within a parent and subsidiary corporate structure, a number of important considerations favor a unified CRP organization:

1. The structure needs to be unified to ensure that significant CRP events (hereinafter 'cases') are reported at all levels on a 'need-to-know' basis in real time. This facilitates simultaneous monitoring of significant incidents and provides for dialogue between parent and subsidiary when circumstances warrant.

2. A unified CRP provides for economies of scale. CRP printed materials, for example, can be designed once by the parent company, printed in volume, and distributed at reduced per unit costs. A CRP information system can also be designed once, built once and used by all units, avoiding unnecessary duplication and ensuring consistency of data.

3. If a third-party vendor is needed, this can be done through a corporate-wide contract that services all

corporate entities. This avoids additional costs and promotes consistency of reporting and allows aggregation of data on a corporate-wide basis.

4. As in case management programs such as workers' compensation or insurance claims, the significance of each CRP incident is typically determined by some type of financial reserve, adjusted from time-to-time given new facts and circumstances, until an ultimate cost is recognized. We used this mechanism for our CRP.

For example, in a case involving a regulatory compliance matter involving billing errors impacting Medicare reimbursement, we would quantify the likely financial exposure and place a reserve accordingly. This approach allowed for prioritization and adjustments of severity on each case and for reporting of aggregate financial exposure to the governing board.

PROGRAM NAME

Ascension Health decided on the name 'Corporate Responsibility Program' (CRP). Another common name is 'Corporate Compliance Program' (CCP). We preferred the former as it suggests a pro-active rather than merely defensive program. Corporate 'response-ability' conveys the notions of civic awareness, attentiveness and responsiveness contributing to the community's benefit. This is particularly apropos for a non-for-profit, charitable corporations such as Ascension Health that provides medical services for the entire community regardless of ability to pay. And yet, for-profit organizations also need to examine and address their responsibilities in their environments and communities as good corporate citizens.

STANDARDS & CODES OF CONDUCT

The foundation of any CRP is the *Vision* and *Mission* of the organization as these are the anchors that articulate and orient the organization as an enterprise and its intended contributions to the community and society. Upon these foundations must rest a set of standards and codes of conduct that each employee needs to understand and abide by.

The governing board and management must take all the time necessary to craft these essential statements, so they effectively describe the values and expectations they have for the organization, themselves and each employee or associate. These enduring and unchangeable foundational statements and standards then need implementation through operating policies and procedures.

For hospitals or any healthcare providers, the following types of standards would be appropriate. This is only illustrative. Each organization must precisely determine the standards applicable to their enterprise.

QUALITY OF CARE

- We treat the person rather than the disease.
- We allow patients to participate in decisions regarding their care by providing them with access to information about their care in a manner that they can understand.

- We respect and maintain the dignity of every patient and strive to provide care in a manner sensitive to cultural differences and individual desires.
- We provide appropriate care based on the patient's medical need, without regard to race, religion, national origin, age, sex, disability, ability to pay or any classification protected by law.
- We provide medically necessary care that is properly documented in the patient's medical record.
- We maintain competencies related to our job responsibilities and exercise appropriate judgment and objectivity when providing patient care.
- We report situations that compromise quality through the appropriate, established channels and correct such situations as soon as possible.

LAWS AND REGULATIONS

- We refrain from any conduct that may violate federal or state laws, including those related to federal program fraud, abuse, and false claims.
- We prohibit any type of payment for or receipt of money or benefits for the purpose of inducing referrals in violation of the anti-kickback statutes.
- We recruit, hire, train, promote, assign, transfer, lay off, recall and terminate associates based on an evaluation of work performance, their own achievements, experience and conduct without regard to race, religion, national origin, age, sex, disability, ability to pay or any classification protected by law.
- We provide associates with the necessary training and education to perform their duties in accordance with applicable laws and regulations.

- We establish relationships only with those individuals or entities who have not been excluded from participation in federal healthcare programs.
- We make certain that reports or other information required to be provided to any federal, state or local government agency are filed accurately and in conformance with the applicable laws and regulations to the best of our knowledge and understanding.
- We do not engage in activities that jeopardize the tax-exempt status of the organization, including certain lobbying and political activities, or activities that further the private or personal interests of an individual rather than our charitable purpose. We refrain from activities that violate the antitrust laws.
- We follow applicable environmental, health and safety requirements in the planning and operation of our facilities.
- We report any practice or condition that we believe may violate laws, rules or regulations, safety standards, internal policies or Standards of Conduct to appropriate levels of management in a timely manner.
- We take steps to ensure that our billing and coding are in compliance with our policies and with federal and state laws and regulations, and are supported by appropriate documentation, including the medical record.

HUMAN RESOURCES

- We do not tolerate any form of harassment or discrimination.
- We seek to be a responsible employer by providing opportunities for professional satisfaction, pride of work and career growth.

- We keep associates informed of activities and events that affect their specific work environment and performance of their job duties.
- We provide training opportunities for associates to assist them in obtaining and maintaining certifications or licensures necessary for the performance of their job duties.
- We maintain a drug free workplace and will not tolerate the use or possession of illegally acquired drugs and/or alcoholic substances while associates are on duty.
- We function in an environmentally responsible manner, providing for the health and safety of our associates as well as our patients and the community.
- We provide a grievance process to report and resolve conflicts without fear of retribution.

BUSINESS & ETHICAL PRACTICES

- We do not engage in unethical or illegal activities in the pursuit of business opportunities.
- We act in good faith and in the best interest of our organization always.
- We appropriately document the care that is provided.
- We submit claims only for medically necessary services and supplies ordered by a physician or legally authorized individual and provided to the patient.
- We do not steal or misappropriate confidential or proprietary information belonging to another person or entity.
- We use resources and assets only to further our Mission.
- We do not use "insider" information for any business outside our organization.
- We do not offer, give, solicit, or receive any form of

bribe, kickback or other improper gift or payment.
- We make certain that payments and other transactions are properly authorized by management and properly documented in the books and records.
- We prepare all financial documents, including financial statements, cost reports, accounting records, expense reports and time sheets accurately.
- We deal with payors and regulatory agencies honestly and accurately.

CONFIDENTIALITY

- We protect and respect the confidentiality of our patients and their medical information.
- We only reveal personal or confidential information concerning patients for legitimate patient care purposes, unless authorized by the patient or otherwise permitted by law.
- We only share confidential information regarding the operations with my associates when they have a legitimate need to know the information to perform their job responsibilities.
- We will take precautions to maintain and manage intellectual property, including patents, trademarks, copyright and software, to protect its value.
- We will maintain confidential information, including financial data and associate information, in a secure manner.

CONFLICTS OF INTEREST

- We avoid engaging in any activity, practice or act that is or appears to be a conflict with the interests.

- We do not solicit or accept money, gifts, favors, services, entertainment, or other things of value unless permitted by organizational policy.
- We abstain from any decision or discussion that might represent a conflict of interest when serving as a member of any outside organization or board.
- We do business only with individuals and companies based on the best interests of the organization.
- We will avoid any appearance of impropriety when dealing with clinicians and referral sources.
- We prohibit the disclosure of proprietary and confidential information related to any unauthorized person or entity, or the use of such information for private benefit.
- We avoid outside employment, consulting arrangements or personal investments if they interfere with our job responsibilities or unduly influence the decisions we are required to make on behalf of our organization.

STATUTES & REGULATIONS

While compliance programs may assume direct responsibility for keeping abreast of current and changing federal, state, local statutory or other external regulatory requirements, at Ascension these were retained by the various departments obliged to conform with such requirements. For example, our Human Resource department professionals kept vigilance over labor laws such as Wage & Hour, IRS, FICA, OSHA, and Workers Compensation. Likewise, Financial Services was responsible for meeting insurance billing and reimbursement regulations set forth by Medicare, Medicaid, and commercial carriers. Should violations occur or alleged, they would become subject to monitoring through the CRP until resolved.

PROGRAM PUBLICATION

I recommend the CRP be memorialized in an associate CRP handbook. This will accomplish three important objectives:

1. This can be used to introduce the program to current and futures associates and encouraged to store them for easy access when needed.
2. This CRP handbook distribution process should include an acknowledgement and receipt form signed and placed in each associates' H.R. personnel file as evidence of their knowledge of standards so they cannot plead ignorance.
3. The handbook should include the anonymous hot-line number and URL for reporting. We put a credit-card size tear out perforation on the back cover that could be removed and placed in a wallet for immediate access.

PROGRAM LAUNCH

Consideration needs to be given to a CRP program launch. The main vehicle used by Ascension was publication and corporate-wide distribution of its nineteen-page CRP handbook that fully described the rationale for CRP, its expectations and all the elements of the program. Each operating units took responsibility of planning and launching their CRP over a specific timeframe.

The primary mode of distribution was during departmental meetings supplemented by individual meetings and news conveyances such as announcements, emails, newsletters, or bulletin boards. In Ascension, this meant that over 100,000 associates, full and part-time, were introduced to the program and received their CRP handbook. Each was required to sign and return an *ACKNOWLEDGEMENT AND RECEIPT* form that was placed in their personnel file.

To accommodate new associates, introduction of CRP was incorporated into the formal orientation process. The CRO may meet with new staff and discusses the program, or a CRP video may also make these introductions.

PERIODIC COMPLIANCE TRAINING

To keep CRP 'top-of-mind', periodic refresher training is necessary. This objective may be accomplished in a number of ways. In our case, I was responsible for the corporate *Human Resources Department* and was asked to initiate a corporate-wide *E-learning* platform to provide this CRP training. We selected and retained an on-line *E-learning IT* partner and developed a series of CRP training modules. With sign-in registrations and pass-word protections, each associate was required to login-in, take the necessary training modules and successfully pass quizzes after completion of each section.

This system allowed the local CRO and their H.R. Dept. and our office to monitor compliance training locally and corporate-wide. Associates were advised that at their annual performance review wage adjustments would be held-up unless and until the CRP refresher training courses were taken and passed. That motivation was effective.

COMPLIANCE OPERATIONS

Beyond governance commitment, setting clear expectations for all associates with ongoing training, CRP operational components include:

1. Non-Retaliation Policy
2. Occurrence Reporting
3. Hot-line Reporting
4. Investigation
5. Remediation
6. Case Management

NON-RETALIATION POLICY

At the outset, to facilitate reporting, it is imperative that associates do not feel duress caused by fear of possible retaliation. There must be a well-publicized and understood *Non-Retaliation Policy*. The idea that a whistleblower is a 'snitch' must be countered aggressively. A contrary view must be promoted and prevail: these CRP reports are courageous acts of loyalty to the organization.

OCCURRENCE REPORTING

CRP is effective only if all associates report actual, suspected, or potential violations in a timely manner. In the hospital setting, this type of practice is well established. 'Incident Reports' are commonly used to document untoward events such as a 'slip & fall' by a patient or visitor, or a medication error. This is vitally important for risk & personnel management and systems improvements. Likewise, CRP needs the same level of acceptance and application.

The normal and preferred mode of reporting is through a direct report or supervisor. When an incident or occurrence is deemed apropos for submission into the CRP, the department enters it officially into the CRP information system and given a case number. Throughout the process of investigation and remediation, the information system will be the tool for periodic reporting updates.

The next and secondary mode of reporting is to an upper level of management where a 'open-door' policy is well established. This should not be used unless there is a significant impediment to normal reporting.

This first and second modes are preferred to the third mode discussed in greater detail below -- anonymous reporting -- for conferring immediately and openly with the associate coming forward is the most efficient method of reporting, investigation, and remediation. This reduces the mystery and enhances credibility that might be suspect when an incident is disclosed secretly and anonymously.

HOT-LINE REPORTING

One reporting mechanism of particular significance is an anonymous hotline independent of the organization. This offers a vital 'safety valve' for an associate not comfortable being identified, or distrustful that they will not face retribution or the scorn of peers, or the incident involves their direct supervisor.

Ascension Health evaluated vendors that operate a 24/7 reporting hotlines that could service all our healthcare ministries in twenty-five states. This was clearly the most economic and effective approach. When receiving calls, hotline attendants invited associates -- but not required it -- to reveal their identities so follow-up was possible. They also assessed the severity and relayed urgent matters immediately to the appropriate contact persons at Ascension.

Even with 100,000+ associates, the aggregate monthly call volume was not significant, less than 100 per month. One unintended consequence was that the hot line was sometimes used for employee complaints that were not compliance issues. Nevertheless, all calls were logged, summarized, and submitted to each operating unit CRP for follow-up. Our office received an aggregate monthly report on all calls. Any we deemed material and not yet reported formally would trigger a follow-up call to that operating unit CRO for clarification.

We also developed a web-based reporting URL if the associate preferred this to a phone call. This had a series of screens for submitting relevant information. The associate was given a PIN and report number so they can periodically check on the status.

INVESTIGATION

The course of investigations of actual and alleged non-compliant occurrences will depend on the facts and circumstances. Most can be managed by internal departmental directors and supervisors. Others require collaboration with other management such as H.R. or internal legal counsel, and sometime external agents such as auditors or law enforcement were brought in.

The important considerations are they are performed competently, thoroughly, confidentially, and timely. The CRO may become involved in the investigation stage or in remediation depending on the severity. In most cases, they may only monitor.

REMEDIATION

Besides prevention and detection, remediation is another critical element of CRP. In violations impacting regulatory bodies, voluntary disclosures may significantly reduce financial consequences and help restore vital relationships. And when corrective measures are taken promptly to rehabilitate or make restitution, these will help repair reputation and restore integrity. Full cooperation and candor are essential.

Internal CRP incidents may be managed in numerous ways depending on if the occurrence involves an individual or group or is a systemic failure whether due to intentional malfeasance or unintentional failure. The investigation needs to determine root causes, so the appropriate remedies are identified, considered, and implemented. These can range from counseling to discipline to termination to involvement of law enforcement involvement; and may require new policies, procedures, training, and system reengineering in cases of systemic failure.

Remediation must include a complete, honest, and candid assessment of 'lesson learned' so, if warranted, they become object lessons that contribute to quality improvement initiatives. Without all these remediation objectives met, the fully potential and value of a CRP will not be achieved. Any attempt to conceal, obscure or 'sugarcoat' a CRP incident is antithetical to the program. CRP requires humility, candor, and honesty.

CASE MANAGEMENT

As in any case management system, a robust information data base is vital. Ascension modeled its program after an insurance claim tracking system. CPR staff worked with its IT department to design a secure internet data base reporting system that each operating unit could securely access and input data for each CRP incident.

Key data input parameters included demographics of date of occurrence, location, department, active status, type of incident, key contact persons and numbers. A summary description of the case was documented. An initial reserve was placed on the case until an investigation began to better understand the scope, significance and likely exposure that would justify raising this reserve. And finally, a logging system allowed for updating facts and circumstances as the case progressed to resolution and the case ultimately closed. The financial reserve resulted in an exact imputed cost to the organization.

This reporting system allowed the parent company to query, sort, aggregate and create reports on a division or corporate-wide basis. This information back-bone was my link to monitor and report on significant cases as well as on corporate trends.

PFIZER PROGRAM

Pfizer, the pharmaceutical company so visible today as the manufacturer of the Covid-19 vaccine has an impressive compliance program that offers another model for aspiring programs developers. They espouse four core values—COURAGE, EXCELLENCE, EQUITY, and JOY. Their publication, *"BLUE BOOK: Pfizer's Code of Conduct"* is available on-line on at the URL: https://cdn.pfizer.com/pfizercom/investors/corporate/Pfizer_2020BlueBook_English.pdf

DISCUSSION

The famous adage, 'an ounce of prevention is worth a pound of cure" precisely describes the intended primary benefit of a sound compliance program. Secondarily, given that a violation or failure has occurred, the system is meant to facilitate prompt detection and remediation.

Peter F. Drucker, regarded the father of modern management, said, 'the leadership is an achievement of trust'. The effective leader understands that trust is not just a personal attribute but needs to be a hallmark of the entire organization if it aspires to corporate excellence. CRP is one vital means to this end. Drucker also said, 'management is doing things right; leadership is doing the right things.' This cannot be achieved without a workforce dedicated to doing things right. This necessitates core values, clear standards, defined codes of conduct, policies and procedures setting expectations and consequences.

Pious pronouncements from executives and a well-constructed compliance program cannot stand alone. These must be supplemented by sound management practices. Principal among these are:

- Prudent hiring practices with background checks
- Secure facilities that protect assets
- Retaining competent independent auditors
- Keeping abreast of regulatory changes
- Sound orientation, training, and certification processes
- Redundancy in procedures that create safeguards
- Consistent and effective supervision

Like effective parenting, a corporate responsibility or compliance program is TOUGH LOVE: set expectations, appeal to 'better angels', be vigilant and follow-through with consequences. These practices when consistently observed will become rooted in the culture; and like a ship's rudder, keep the corporation moving steadily on its proper course.

PERSPECTIVES

MY LIFE, TIMES & CONVICTIONS

CHAPTER VII

50 SHADES OF TRUMP

Litany of Personality Flaws

CONTENTS

Preface.. 156
Contagious... 158
Narcissist... 159
Stupid.. 160
Unrepentant.. 161
Crude... 162
Dumb... 162
Crazed... 163
Insincere.. 164
Impudent... 165
Vain... 165
Unfaithful.. 166
Sanctimonious.. 167
Duplicitous... 167
Repetitive... 168
Insidious... 169
Greedy.. 169
Lethal.. 170
Dangerous.. 171
Bluster.. 172
Indolent.. 172
Impudent.. 173
Undisciplined... 174
Pompous.. 175
Stingy... 176
Audacious.. 177
Whiner... 178
Vindictive... 179
Cheater.. 180

Vile	181
Craven	182
Racist	183
Ignorant	184
Misogynist	185
Maladroit	186
Phony	187
Impervious	188
Fabricator	189
Obstreperous	190
Dogmatic	191
Hypocritical	192
Unscrupulous	192
Boring	193
Braggart	194
Jaundiced	195
Pampered	195
Fixated	196
Disloyal	197
Impetuous	198
Pathetic	199
Afterword	200

50 SHADES OF TRUMP
LITANY OF PERSONALITY FLAWS

PREFACE

I had the privilege of serving in leadership capacities in U.S. hospitals and multi-hospital systems for thirty years. I was fortunate to become a hospital CEO at age 29 and so faced the challenges of senior leadership my entire career. Over that period, my leadership skills were tested, and through successes and failures learned about leadership. Now retired, I decided to share my hard-earned perspectives on Donald Trump as leader.

After enduring four tortuous years of Donald J. Trump who has already pegged by presidential historians as among the ten least effective of the forty-six American presidents, this litany of fifty-character traits that, when combined, offer a partial accounting of Trump's unique genetically informed and experientially acquired personality attributes that inspired such malfeasance.

Devoid of precious few redeeming qualities as a person, celebrity, or leader, that Trump would morph into 'Trumpism' is nothing less than an American tragedy. Like polluted lakes, it will be decades before our civil society can clean the putrid residue of his impact on American norms and attitudes. The clearest example is the normalization of falsehoods. The "Big Lie," that he did not actually loose the 2020 presidential election, is at the apex of his incredible capacity to deceive, distort and denounce.

Whether by pure political party fealty, inconceivable naivete or devilish disregard for science, facts, or evidence, that over thirty percent to Americans continue to cling to Trump's coattails even in defeat is remarkable and, to our grave peril, a continuing threat to democracy writ large.

For the sixty percent or so of Americans who see Trump in the true light of day, these fifty shades of Trump will not be surprising. If this litany in a modest way serves as a checklist of warning signs to measure future presidential candidates, let us hope it serves a constructive purpose and not simply a regrettable recitation of an American electoral failure.

Even though I has drawn this list from my personal observations from afar -- as a keen American expatriate observer living in Bangkok, Thailand -- they seem to parallel much of the professional wisdom and insights of Mary Lea Trump, the niece of the former president Donald Trump, who has been critical of Trump applying her keen insights from her personal encounters in the Trump family combined with deep insights as a PhD in psychology. My own master's degree in Counseling was another informed source for this work.

Like a dangerous medical condition, the more Americans understand the symptoms that inspired Trumpism, the greater the possibility it can and will be contained and, hopefully, eradicated like polio, measles, and Covid-19, from the political mainstream sooner rather than later.

And to assure literal precision in this litany, I have enlisted one of the most respected conventional sources of language meaning, the Merriam-Webster Dictionary.

CONTAGIOUS

contagious adjective

🔖 Save Word

con·ta·gious | \ kən-ˈtā-jəs 🔊 \

Definition of *contagious*
1 : transmissible by direct or indirect contact with an infected person

An epidemiologist will tell you that a "host" -- in their parlance -- means a carrier of disease. While relevant when discussing parasitic, bacterial, and viral agents, this is an apt metaphor for anyone in a position of authority that hosts rallies to spread vile insults, discernable lies and hateful provocations spreading misery on the body politic. Considering the enormous reach of social media that amplifies these hateful messages, Trump has outdone the last expert at spreading contagion, Adolf Hitler.

A once in a century pandemic and once in over two centuries (since April 30, 1789) presidential misfit has crippled our country. That a significant segment of the U.S. electorate does not recognize, admit this appalling state of disability has become the nerve-racking existential threat to our beloved U.S. democracy.

Unfortunately, one of the few areas of expertise Trump has raised to an art form is propaganda. Not since the Nazi Joseph Goebbels who said, "If you repeat a lie often enough, people will believe it, and you will even come to believe it yourself," has a political leader so mesmerized his base with fiction and mischief and self-righteous contempt for opponents, government institutions, huge segment of society, our allies and even the earth we live on. What he coined 'China-virus' is better renamed as the 'Trump-plague.' His contagion is even worse as it has put not just our health but our government and society in the ICU.

NARCISSTIC

narcissist noun

🔖 Save Word

nar·cis·sist | \ ˈnär-sə-sist 🔊 \
plural **narcissists**

Definition of *narcissist* (Entry 1 of 2)

: an individual showing symptoms of or affected by narcissism: such as

a : an extremely self-centered person who has an exaggerated sense of self-importance

His affect, words and deeds all testify to his gross self-absorption. Trump, not the sun, is the center of our solar system in his estimation. Just listen to him. He wears this mantle of superiority like a badge, and it informs his every thought and calculation.

While narcissist is a highfalutin term for 'ego-tripper' it is also is clinical jargon for a diagnosable personality disorder. Undoubtedly, Trump never allowed a psychiatrist anywhere near him to make this type of clinical evaluation and a diagnosis official. So, the word used here admits no clinical authority or attribution but simply a label that fits Trump perfectly based on countless hours of disgusting observations.

Somehow, he melded this gross narcissism with scant personal charm that enthralls so many. The Apprentice lionized his executive prowess. Such is the stuff of celebrity, but this has been a catastrophe as he gutted the foundations of public service in a country that Lincoln declared was a government "of the people, by the people and for the people." Trump has recalibrated this noble state into "a government of Trump, by Trump and for Trump." How else would a narcissist behave?

STUPID

stupid adjective

🔖 Save Word

stu·pid | \ 'stü-pəd 🔊, 'styü- \

Definition of *stupid* (Entry 1 of 2)

1. **a** : slow of mind : OBTUSE
   b : given to unintelligent decisions or acts : acting in an unintelligent or careless manner
   c : lacking intelligence or reason : BRUTISH

2. : dulled in feeling or sensation : TORPID
   // still *stupid* from the sedative

While Trump acolytes consider him a political and public relations genius, and even though his detractors marvel at his sinister cleverness, he is stupid intellectually. Poorly read, academically unprepared and with questionable literary aptitude, for ascension to such a prominent position of responsibility and world leadership, he is remarkably inept, and it showed. In plain view, his strong preferences for TV cable news, obsessive Twitter feeds, and proven appetite for short bites of information rather than delve into conventional written reports of substance, his lacks the mental rigor and truncated attention span resemble an adolescent in middle school, anything but serious executive.

Indisputable evidence of his subpar mental capacity is reveled when comparing his prepared teleprompter polished speeches, written by staff, with to his 'ad-lib' remarks, rants and digressions filled with repetitive cliches, poor pronunciations, illogic, and street jargon. And since his communications are full hyperbole and outright lies, this too hardly reflects a man of learning. Stupid and moronic is more like it.

UNREPENTANT

unrepentant adjective

🔖 Save Word

un·re·pen·tant | \ ˌən-ri-ˈpen-tənt 🔊 \

Definition of *unrepentant*

1 : not feeling or exhibiting shame or remorse : not <u>repentant</u>
// an *unrepentant* sinner

2 : feeling or showing no inclination to change : <u>UNAPOLOGETIC</u>

The word 'sorry' is nowhere in Trump's lexicon or in his heart. 'Doubling-down' on behaviors and insidious comments others would humbly admit as mistakes is unbecoming of him. His classic 'modus operandi' is to deny and obfuscate any responsibility for error. He simply cannot accept this is possible.

Mary Trump, his niece, has often cited Trump's incredible fear of failure as the source of his defensive armor denying any wrongdoing, misstep, or mistake. This lack of self-awareness, self-correction, or readiness to improve is dangerous in leadership.

To become president of the United States, assume such grave responsibilities without any government experience, surround himself with unprepared appointed advisors with a tendency to ignore advisors who are experts, and unwilling to "learn on the job" or make course corrections along the way is a recipe for governance gone astray. For us, failures are opportunities for learning and improvements; for Trump, it is above his paygrade to make mistakes.

This is exactly what occurred during the Trump presidency. To retain or restore political power, his Republican party prefers to celebrate rather than castigate such malfeasance. They became complicit as not to incur the rath of Trump and his followers.

CRUDE

crude *adjective*

🔖 Save Word

\ ˈkrüd 🔊 \
cruder; crudest

Definition of *crude* (Entry 1 of 2)

1 : marked by the primitive, gross, or elemental or by uncultivated simplicity or vulgarity

In October 2016, the *Washington Post* revealed Trump's verbatim, gross, and lewd discussion about women during his candidacy. What was as shocking as his crude dialogue was that it did nothing to detract from his appeal or ultimate success. This was not an uncharacteristic aberration; it exposed Trump's unabashed vulgarity that he is known to display in private conversations and often the centerpiece of his public oratory. His jaded followers seem to revel in this vulgarity.

His base seems to revel in his crudeness. His 'street-talk' vulgarity spices up his equally inappropriate remarks and insults. These are the unmistakable characteristics of the form and substance of a Trump rally. Not since Jerry Springer has crude depravity so captivated crowds.

DUMB

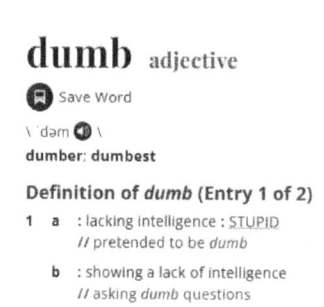

dumb *adjective*

🔖 Save Word

\ ˈdəm 🔊 \
dumber; dumbest

Definition of *dumb* (Entry 1 of 2)

1 a : lacking intelligence : STUPID
    // pretended to be *dumb*
   b : showing a lack of intelligence
    // asking *dumb* questions
    // a *dumb* look on his face

Dumb is closely related to stupidity which is more a manifestation of 'dumb-ness,' Trump seems to function not on any intellectual plane, but from a more confined cerebral space governed by appetites, accolades and presumptions found in the most uncritical, unscrupulous, and biased sources like Fox News opinion pundits and extremist advisors.

There is little evidence that he filters his obnoxious pronouncements with the least bit of intellectual rigor. And he is certainly not known for his mental brilliance despite pronouncing himself among the smartest people on earth.

Dumb is not a kind term for a presidential term, yet it fits. In press conferences, he could barely field policy questions. His inexperience and lack of preparation showed; his answers were typically cliches indicating scant depth of understanding. They were often half-truths or outright lies, turning answers into sound bites of self-promotion.

CRAZED

craze verb

Save Word

\ 'krāz \
crazed; crazing; crazes

Definition of *craze* (Entry 1 of 2)
transitive verb
1 : to make insane or as if insane

A majority of sane Americans who observe Trump are eft with a sense of disbelief and disgust. They also have seen this absurd MAGA craziness overtake family, friends, and associates. This insanity has been called a 'parallel universe' or an 'alternate reality' perpetrated by copious amounts of falsehoods repeated, ad nauseum, on Twitter, other social media, and cable outlets until believed as gospel truth rather than pulp fiction. This inability to see reality is downright insane. The Republican lens is truly distorted.

His crazed declarations of the "Big Lie" may become known as the 'coup de grace' that destroyed democracy in the U.S. No amount of logic, contrary court decisions, or common sense has dented this fantasy.

The "Big Lie' is a rabid dog on the loose biting everyone close and rendering our democracy weak, feverish with hallucinations and turning to paralysis leading to certain death.

INSINCERE

insincere adjective

Save Word

in·sin·cere | \ ˌin-sin-ˈsir, -sən- \

Definition of *insincere*

: not sincere : HYPOCRITICAL

The *Oxford English Dictionary* offers insight on the word sincere. "Sincere," it states, was first recorded in English in the 1530s from the Latin word *sincerus*, meaning "clean, pure, sound." Precious few have ever used any of these words to describe Trump or his business practices and later, his presidency.

The gaudy pretense of the Trump brand makes no claim on sincerity anyway. He prefers audacity to purity or simplicity. Cleverness, cunning and deception characterize his methods. Insincerity is a hallmark of his life script. For Trump, it has been a key to his perverted understanding of how to achieve success.

IMPUDENT

impudent adjective

🔖 Save Word

im·pu·dent | \ ˈim-pyə-dənt 🔊 \

Definition of *impudent*

1 : marked by <u>contemptuous</u> or <u>cocky</u> boldness or disregard of others : <u>INSOLENT</u>

2 *obsolete* : lacking <u>modesty</u>

When I was a child watching Saturday morning wresting, the antics displayed were so outrageous even then I sensed they had to be bold theatrics, not true tests of athletic prowess. I presumed the winning wrestler preordained in the rehearsal ring. Yet even today, avid fans of this kind of sport abound. Go figure.

Trump has deployed similar tactics to excite and motivate equally gullible cohorts of followers who either feed on this distortion or claim to be true believers. His zealous rhetoric spares nobody in this 'crosshairs.' His bold immodest pronouncements and vile insults humiliate opponents and whole classes of people. His faithful chat slogans that amplify and legitimize taunts.

VAIN

vain adjective

🔖 Save Word

\ ˈvān 🔊 \

Definition of *vain*

1 : having or showing undue or excessive <u>pride</u> in one's appearance or achievements : <u>CONCEITED</u>

The Trump hairdo says it all, his signature badge of vanity. Partially bald like his father, Fred, Trump has concealed his unseemly receding hairline with a self-inflicted coiffeur remedy. This is just the proverbial 'tip of the ice-berg.' Vanity is his crowning attribute reflected in his lifestyle, brand, decorating, propaganda, demeanor, and self-concept.

A secondary definition of vain also applies in spades. Trump's business failures – 'in vain attempts' -- are so well documented and yet earnestly concealed, that unsuccess is one of his distinguishing legacies as a business executive, and not recognized nor acknowledged by his followers

UNFAITHFUL

unfaithful adjective

🔖 Save Word

un·faith·ful | \ ˌən-ˈfāth-fəl 🔊 \

Definition of *unfaithful*

: not faithful:

a : not adhering to vows, allegiance, or duty : DISLOYAL
// an *unfaithful* friend

b : not faithful to marriage vows
// suspected her husband of being *unfaithful*

c : INACCURATE, UNTRUSTWORTHY
// an *unfaithful* copy of a document

Marital infidelity is old news with Trump. Melania is the latest victim. She stoically bares the stigma of a woman scorned by public humiliation. But Trump's trail of unfaithfulness goes far beyond the bedroom. Banks, business associates, former friends, contract workers, employees and now the American people have been stung by Trump's unfaithfulness. The U.S. Constitution that he swore to honor and uphold is victim also.

His "Big Lie" is his deadliest manifestation of infidelity. His cohort of Republican followers have joined in a parade of legislative measures that reinforce this blatant disregard for democratic electoral norms to keep or restore their political advantage at any cost, even at the price of loss of integrity, the aftermath and stain of infidelity.

SANCTIMONIOUS

sanctimonious adjective

🔖 Save Word

sanc·ti·mo·nious | \ ˌsaŋ(k)-tə-ˈmō-nē-əs 🔊, -nyəs \

Definition of *sanctimonious*

1 : hypocritically pious or devout

His pseudo-reverence for things biblical has somehow cemented his base with a vast number of white Evangelicals. They have been oblivious to a host of un-Christ-like attitudes, policies, and behaviors. This has been one of the tragic sub-plots of the Trump era; the cooption of the religious right. It is unlikely Trump supports Evangelical views out of conviction; it is expediency only. That one demographic, if reborn as independents, could upend Trump world faster than a baptism by immersion.

DUPLICITOUS

duplicitous adjective

🔖 Save Word

du·plic·i·tous | \ dü-ˈpli-sə-təs 🔊 *also* dyü- \

Definition of *duplicitous*

: marked by duplicity : deceptive in words or action
// *duplicitous* tactics

For Trump duplicity is just another valid personal and profession negotiating tactic and business practice. Without an ethical core, Trump has stiffed so many through duplicitous dealing. Banks and the IRS are the most aggrieved by his duplicity. It is becoming clearer and clearer from revelations about the Trump organizations dual bookkeeping schemes until now concealed at all costs, his blatant duplicity in reporting his financial condition may finally catch up with him. Let us hope so.

Charles M. Blow of the *New York Times* warned us back in Aug. 31, 2016, in an article entitled, *"The Duplicity of Donald Trump."* He finished his prescient opinion piece this way, "this is what every voter must remember: Trump has two faces and two sets of facts and too much latitude to spread his animus, anti-intellectualism and lies, and he must never see the inside of the Oval Office." What a shame that not enough of the U.S. electorate heeded Mr. Blow's sage warning.

REPETITIVE

repetitive adjective

Save Word

re·pet·i·tive | \ ri-ˈpe-tə-tiv \

Definition of *repetitive*

1 : REPETITIOUS

The gifted Roman orator Cicero would have turned over in his grave at each Trump rally had he been near them. Trump's stump speeches are repetitious rantings of mostly insults, false claims, ego-enhancing declarations and boasts. There is nothing oratorically satisfying about them. One of his obnoxious tendencies to repeat slogans, insults and lies like a favorite hits album.

INSIDIOUS

insidious adjective

🔖 Save Word

in·sid·i·ous | \ in-ˈsi-dē-əs 🔊 \

> **Essential Meaning of** *insidious*
> *formal* : causing harm in a way that is gradual or not easily noticed

Trump's political harm includes coziness to dictators and hostility toward perennial allies. His cronies have wreaked havoc in all areas of the federal government. Revelations have surfaced on how his devious schemes wormed into the government through insidious means not subject to scrutiny or condemnation.

This disrupted civility and shattered norms within our national bureaucracy causing mass resignations and deep ruptures in morale in career workers. From diplomats to technicians to attorneys, Trump's political cronies have polluted the body politic.

In March 2018, *ProRepubica* reported, "At least 187 Trump political appointees have been federal lobbyists, and despite President Trump's campaign pledge to 'drain the swamp,' many are now overseeing the industries they once lobbied on behalf of. We've also discovered ethics waivers that allow Trump staffers to work on subjects in which they have financial conflicts of interest."

GREEDY

greedy adjective

🔖 Save Word

\ ˈgrē-dē 🔊 \
greedier; greediest

Definition of *greedy*

1 : marked by greed : having or showing a selfish desire for wealth and possessions

His need to amass fortunes and brag about it is one of his passions. Trump's business schemes are dedicated to maximizing profits with scant regard for delivering a reputable product or service. Lawsuits from aggrieved clients such as the successful court findings concerning the now defunct *Trump University* testify to Trump's avarice. His overpriced hotel rooms, slopping bookkeeping and routine stiffing contractors and employees prove his overriding interest of amassing wealth.

LETHAL

lethal adjective
Save Word
le-thal | \ 'lē-thəl \
Definition of *lethal* (Entry 1 of 2)
1 a : of, relating to, or causing death
      // death by *lethal* injection

Trump unquestionably instigated the January 6th invasion of the capital resulting in deaths, disabilities, and destruction. Whether Trump, going forward, suffers civil or criminal consequences is not yet determined, but he is deserving of recrimination on all counts. Those who look to shield, deny, or obfuscate his moral and rhetorical culpability have decided to abet this abhorrent conduct that inspired such devastation.

Trump used his capacity to be lethal in the realm of government writ large. Significant programs were dealt death blows by executive order. Competent public servants were axed, demoted, or demoralized by political mischief.

In terms of death toll, his greatest achievement was in trivializing and politicizing the deadly Covid-19 pandemic. To make public health a political ploy cost countless lives and untold morbidity. Trump faithful went to their deaths proclaiming, with their last breaths, freedom of choice, rejecting mandates that required wearing masks in public or vaccination that surely could have saved them. And for a confirmed germaphobe, Trump continued to hold rallies without no regard for the risks of viral transmission.

DANGEROUS

dangerous adjective

Save Word

dan·ger·ous | \ ˈdān-jə-rəs ; ˈdān-jərs, -zhrəs \

Definition of *dangerous*

1 : involving possible injury, pain, harm, or loss : characterized by danger
// a *dangerous* job

Danger comes in multiple forms beyond what is the purely lethal. Environmental degradation, civil unrest, international turmoil are forms of danger that Trump willingly perpetrated by omission and commission. His abrupt reneging on the Paris Climate accord and departure from the Iran Nuclear Deal are prime examples of how Trump destabilized and harmed our national interests and unilaterally flaunted disregard for our allies.

His championing white supremacists destabilized civility at home. The revelations about General Mark Milley reassuring our adversaries during the election denial turmoil further attests to how dangerous Trump was in the final days of the presidential transition.

Regrettably, even with after a Biden victory, the danger posed by Trumpian political antics in 2022 and 2024 resembles a hurricane churning offshore, building force, and heading toward our shores.

BLUSTER

bluster verb

🔖 Save Word

blus·ter | \ ˈblə-stər 🔊 \
blustered; blustering \ ˈblə-st(ə-)riŋ 🔊 \

Definition of *bluster* (Entry 1 of 2)

intransitive verb

1 : to talk or act with noisy <u>swaggering</u> threats
   // brags and *blusters* but rarely does what he says he'll do

    No one since P.T. Barnum has someone used hyperbole to greater effect. Trump has outdone himself with self-aggrandizing boasts. From crowd sizes to personal brilliance to his self-assessed grandiose presidential ranking, Trump has canonized himself a saint on every measure. Clearly recognized as pure B.S. by a majority of American; yet, about a third of the citizenry have accepted this bluster as unshakable truths and worship at his altar, nonetheless.

INDOLENT

indolent adjective

🔖 Save Word

in·do·lent | \ ˈin-də-lənt 🔊 \

Definition of *indolent*

1   a   : <u>averse</u> to activity, effort, or movement : habitually lazy
      b   : showing an inclination to laziness
          // an *indolent* sigh

Aside from golf courses and dinner tables and his Twitter account, Trump has proven prone to lethargy. For a president with worldwide, complex responsibilities, his schedule hardly reflects the enormity of the challenges at hand. His lack of attention span, preference for cable news rather than digesting full briefings, and jaw-dropping dismissal of cogent arguments from advisors he does not want to hear or agree with confirms his indolent nature and conduct.

No wonder his personal businesses failed so often. Without discipline, diligence, and perseverance, he lacks these essential qualities of an effective chief executive officer, and he brought this same mediocrity into the White House. He became an embarrassment to not only most Americans but to our allies around the world.

It is difficult to overstate how his self-centeredness and his lethargic nature devastated the federal government's performance related to crises from hurricanes relief to pandemic. response. His instinct was to avoid political fallout rather than address problems promptly and vigorously.

IMPUDENT

impudent adjective

Save Word

im·pu·dent | \ ˈim-pyə-dənt \

Definition of *impudent*
1 : marked by contemptuous or cocky boldness or disregard of others : INSOLENT
2 *obsolete* : lacking modesty

Except for Vladimir Putin and Kim Jong-Un, no person or institution escaped his disdain. The institutions of government reviled and held in contempt. His advisors expected to kowtow to him. This was at the top of their position descriptions. Only 'yes-men' and 'yes-women' could thrive or survive in his presence. Cogent counter arguments dismissed as disloyal.

He paraded his contempt on his shirt sleeve. He took the same petty family owned "I'm the boss" affect into the executive branch. Teamwork was rare and rarely encouraged. Respect for the 'separation of powers' as a constitutional mandate was eschewed repeatedly throughout his presidency. He boldly deployed *Department of Justice* to do his political bidding and his personal lawyers did all they could to disrupt or deny inter-governmental cooperation or communication.

UNDISCIPLINED

undisciplined adjective

Save Word

un·dis·ci·plined | \ ən- di-sə-plənd \

Definition of *undisciplined*

: lacking in discipline or self-control
// *undisciplined* behavior
// an unruly and *undisciplined* child

His penchant for fast-foods and copious hours digesting cable news betray a habitual 'couch potato.' He was not willing to set and adhere to a normal routine executive schedule becoming of a world leader. His lackadaisical daily schedule and preference for golf course carts underscores how a pampered, wealthy man finds it almost impossible, at age 70 plus, to change habits required to meet the rigors of the Oval Office.

His inability to even read daily briefs and a lack of patience in meetings are undeniable evidence that he could not accommodate even the most rudimentary demands of his office. It was merely the glory and prestige of the office, not the opportunity to serve the public good, that fueled his presidential ambitions.

Another telltale indicator of his lack of discipline, not to mention his shallow analytical skills, were on display daily whenever required to comment on complex policy matters or pressing events. His replies were typical full of cliches, twisted for self-aggrandizement and short on substance. While his affect was one of confidence, a discerning audience could detect how this façade concealed little preparation or command of facts.

POMPOUS

pompous adjective

Save Word

pomp·ous | \ ˈpäm-pəs \

Definition of *pompous*

1 : excessively elevated or ornate
   // *pompous* rhetoric

2 : having or exhibiting self-importance : ARROGANT
   // a *pompous* politician

No word conjures up the beloved tale by Danish author Hans Christian Anderson's, "The Emperor's New Clothes," than the word 'pompous.' It is uncharitable yet tempting to suspect that Anderson had Donald J. Trump in his imagination as he penned this classic. Imagine the 6'3", 244-pound Trump prancing down

Pennsylvania Avenue with his self-satisfied grin swaggering from side to side embracing his adoring crowd lining the avenue.

Suddenly, a small child of ten bolts from the onlookers. He stops about twenty feet ahead of Trump. Just before the Secret Service catch-up to remove him, he points directly at Trump's belly and cries out, "Look, President Trump isn't got clothes on!!" Aghast, the crowd begins to see the truth of this bold comment with their own eyes and their cheers morph into dull booing. The Trump brands begins to tarnish before their eyes.

Bewildered, Trump looks down and sees his hairy bulbous midriff that obstructs notice of his chubby bare legs and feet below. His grin becomes a scowl. Melanie smartly pulls her shawl from her shoulder and barely covers Donald's private parts as they await a limo to rescue them from brutal embarrassment.

STINGY

stingy adjective

Save Word

stin·gy | \ 'stin-jē \
stingier; stingiest

Definition of *stingy*

1 : not generous or liberal : sparing or scant in using, giving, or spending
   // *stingy* with the salt
   // *stingy* employee benefits

2 : meanly scanty or small
   // *stingy* portions of meat

Nothing typifies Trump's stinginess more than the saga of his disgraced and now defunct Trump Foundation via court-supervised dissolution in 2019. Using charitable funds for personal and political purposes blatantly violated its charter. While claiming to be philanthropic at heart, his actions belie the boast: par for the course in Trump-world.

The most egregious and pernicious examples of his stinginess is failure to pay employees, lawyers, contractors and other outstanding compensation or debts owed. For Trump, debts are not obligations, they are sport for denying and denigrating. This conduct construed as shrewd business practice in the Trump organization.

Stingy is a business ethic for Trump. His niggardly attitude is symptomatic of his lack of compassion or honor as he wallows in his self-centered world of entitlement. To fully harness the impact and stinginess, his bevy of lawyers countersue to overwhelm and overcome any recourse for victims in pursuit to redress damages Trump meted out.

AUDACIOUS

audacious adjective

Save Word

au·da·cious | \ ȯ-ˈdā-shəs \

Definition of *audacious*

1. a : intrepidly daring : ADVENTUROUS
    // an *audacious* mountain climber
   b : recklessly bold : RASH
    // an *audacious* maneuver
2. : contemptuous of law, religion, or decorum : INSOLENT
    // an *audacious* maverick

Audacity is his badge of honor. He enjoys displaying it fearlessly like a circus clown. The Trump brand, his properties, his demeanor all portray in-your-face audacity. Only the best, the most pretentious, the gaudy will do.

His inaugural address audaciously proclaimed, "Together we will determine the course of America and the world for years to come." The tragic result of four years fulfilled the prediction. He crippled America's standing in the world with his audacious confrontations with our allies. He ruptured accords. He alienated without hesitation with his brutish and arrogant style.

His audacious pandering to Kim Jong-un and Vladimir Putin confounded American foreign policy. Our allies grew to disdain his arrogance. Trust, consistency and honoring our commitments are essential for stable foreign relationships. He managed to destroy our reputation for years to come in the eyes of the world.

WHINER

whine verb

Save Word

\ ˈ(h)wīn \
whined; whining

Definition of *whine* (Entry 1 of 2)

intransitive verb

1   a   : to utter a high-pitched plaintive or distressed cry
     b   : to make a sound similar to such a cry
        // the wind *whined* in the chimney

2   : to complain with or as if with a whine
     // always *whining* about the weather

He has made self-pity an artform. Petulant and peevish to a fault, any slight is immediately countered with hostility. His rallies often dwell on perceived or actual slights. Political opponents are personal enemies. He complains about any justifiable criticism and declares it 'fake news' or spews some alternative facts that are actually fantasy harnessed to dismiss unflattering truths.

Shades of Trump are infantile, normally found in babes and youngsters who have yet to mature and shed these less productive coping behaviors in favor of more emotionally rewarding responses. Whining is the most elemental of these childish ways and Trump resorts to this constantly when aggrieved.

The "Big Lie" was simply the culmination of his whining. Now, a chorus of followers and Republican legislators parrot this tune and use it to corrupt electoral processes themselves.

VINDICTIVE

vindictive adjective
Save Word

vin·dic·tive | \ vin-ˈdik-tiv \

Definition of *vindictive*

1   a   : disposed to seek revenge : VENGEFUL
    b   : intended for or involving revenge

2   : intended to cause anguish or hurt : SPITEFUL

Do not ever cross Trump. Striking back is instinctive like breathing for Trump. He is most ingenious and willing to spend profusely to discredit, disarm and punish detractors; the notion of forgiveness as foreign as speaking Swahili.

One needs a calculator to compute the number of know public persona who became victim of his vengeance during his presidency. Add to these scores of others who came before in his business and private dealings and the numbers might astound us. His vindictiveness has no end. Unless you supplicate before him on bended knees, there is still a 50-50 chance this will not suffice.

CHEATER

cheater noun

🔖 Save Word

cheat·er | \ ˈchē-tər 🔊 \
plural **cheaters**

Definition of *cheater*

1 : one who cheats: such as

   a : one who violates rules dishonestly
      // a *cheater* at cards
      // tax *cheaters*

Most people caught cheating in their youth are so embarrassed as to never indulge in this vice again. How Trump learned that cheating was a perfectly acceptable business practice is credited to his father, Fred. Well documented are multiple incidences where Trump cheated or reneged in business dealings; so well, that the citizens the New York city used the term 'con-man' when referring to Trump; unfortunately, word did not spread widely enough in the U.S. electorate.

Trump's public relations machine manufactured his celebrity and contrived legendary status perpetuated by fifteen seasons of "The Apprentice." This wove a completely different fabric of Trumpian business acumen. In typical Hollywood mythical fashion, his contrived prowess overtook gullible viewers' imaginations and Trump rode this concoction of B.S. into the White House.

Cheating Joe Biden of his closely won presidential election was simply the latest and yet most tragic cheating scheme of Trumps. Trump has now joined the world's strongmen and tyrants in his bid to stay in power. His contempt for democracy boggles the mind and yet inspires a political cult he has carefully groomed.

VILE

vile adjective

Save Word

\ 'vī(-ə)l \
viler \ 'vī-lər \; **vilest** \ 'vī-ləst \

Definition of *vile*

1   **a** : morally despicable or abhorrent
// nothing is so *vile* as intellectual dishonesty

      b : physically repulsive : FOUL
// a *vile* slum

Speaking of calculation, the catalog of vile comments and deeds in four years of the Trump presidency will never be equaled. From insults to a Gold-Star Family, to his absurdly hurtful comments about John McCain's capture, to allowing separation of youngsters from their mothers at the Southern border, Trump's vile conduct is well documented. For him, *Making America Great Again* was justification for inhuman personal discourse and policy decisions that only a vile persona could conjure up or condone abetted by an equally cynical set of advisors like the dour Stephen Miller.

Convictions anyone may have had that America is a cradle of compassion and human rights dispelled forever in his four years of callous disregard for minorities, women's rights, the underprivileged and immigrants. With gusto, he generated scorn around the world. His contempt for the environment by gutting regulations and pulling out of the Paris Climate Accord extended his villainy beyond humanity to include mother earth. His dismissing medical and scientific advice was routine and emphatic. His alternative unproven remedies for mitigating Covid-19 earned him bragging rights as a vile quack.

CRAVEN

craven adjective

🔖 Save Word

cra·ven | \ ˈkrā-vən 🔊 \

Definition of *craven*

1 : lacking the least bit of courage : contemptibly fainthearted
  // ... *craven* mercenaries who would not fight ...
  — Thomas Fleming

2 *archaic* : DEFEATED, VANQUISHED

Despite a façade bravado, Trump is a wimp at heart. The shades of Trump and consequent deeds they evoke support this fact. Principal among his cravenness is his dodging the military draft by devious cheating. Also, absent wealth and the backing from 'daddy' when in dire financial straits, his string of bankruptcies should have dealt mortal blows to his reputation and fortune.

It was not courage or intelligence that gave him 'nine-lives,' it is cunning, depravity and craven disregard for truth and the law whenever convenient and opportunistic. Hallmarks of a conman.

A mob bosses has underlings do their 'dirty work.' Trump does not toil or get his hands dirty either. Ask Michael Cohen. And do not count on Trump to 'have your back.' Only one back matters to him, his own. Loyalty and reciprocity do not coexist in Trump world. How someone that craven can be so venerated by so many is astounding. That he can overtake a national political party and prod state legislatures to do his bidding is equally astounding. It certainly smacks of how the Mafia successfully infiltrates unions to perpetuate their racketeering. The rot must be eradicated.

RACIST

racist adjective

🔖 Save Word

rac·ist | \ ˈrā-sist 🔊 *also* -shist \

Definition of *racist* (Entry 1 of 2)

: of, relating to, or characterized by <u>racism</u>: such as

a : having, reflecting, or fostering the belief that race (see <u>RACE entry 1 sense 1a</u>) is a fundamental determinant of human traits and capacities and that racial differences produce an inherent superiority of a particular race

The least disputed shade of Trump is his deep-seated and long-standing racism. In 1973, Trump and company was sued by the Department of Justice for housing discrimination against African American renters. Trump ranted about Barack Obama's citizenship. He castigated Mexican immigrants repeatedly. On and on, in word and deed, his contempt for minorities led his propaganda script.

And the corollary to this, white supremacist sympathies, exacerbated these racial stereotypes and insults. This animus in a country so diversified, founded by cohorts of immigrants from nations around the world, has created an extreme chasm of hatred and bigotry he stirred up and fomented.

Instead of celebrating America unique diversity as a strength and source of cultural richness, he turned the conversation into taunts about threats, rapes, criminality, and white grievance.

He delegitimized the "Black Lives Matter" movement by obstruction and demonization through contrary hype that only propagated falsehoods and propped up the resolve of white supremacists and white sympathizers who were typically an uneducated minority lacking in racial empathy.

IGNORANT

ignorant adjective

🔖 Save Word

ig·no·rant | \ ˈig-n(ə-)rənt 🔊 \

Definition of *ignorant*

1   a   : destitute of knowledge or education
         // an *ignorant* society
       also : lacking knowledge or comprehension of the thing specified
         // parents *ignorant* of modern mathematics
    b   : resulting from or showing lack of knowledge or intelligence
         // *ignorant* errors

Learning was never a strong suite for Trump. He lacked the diligence, patience, and aptitude. He preferred to excel through cunning and depended on the luxury of inherited wealth to seek an identity and achieve fame. He did learn from Father Fred how to connive, cheat and renege. But as for intellectual pursuits, the "Twitter King" found no time for delving into substantive matters.

Advisors coached on how to 'spoon-feed' information to Trump to not bore him or overwhelm him with details. His level of comprehension was commensurate with on his puny attention span. Consequently, he never spoke as if he had a command of any complex subject. Usually, his comments were cliché like, skimmed the surface with no depth of understanding.

Those who remember Archie Bunker will recognize he was the fictional TV prototype for Trump. The principal difference being Archie was 'blue collar' while Trump 'white collar.' Character traits of Bunker noted by *Wikipedia* eerily resemble Trump: "Archie has a gruff, overbearing demeanor, largely defined by his bigotry towards a diverse group of individuals: Black people, Hispanics, "Commies", gay people, hippies, Jews, Asians, Catholics, "women's libbers." Trump is Bunker reincarnate.

MISOGYNIST

misogynist noun

Save Word

mi·sog·y·nist | \ mə-ˈsä-jə-nist \
plural **misogynists**

Definition of *misogynist* **(Entry 1 of 2)**
: a person who hates or discriminates against women : a misogynistic person

This is old news too. Who can forget the Access Hollywood episode? If Trump did not inspire coining the term "trophy wife," he could have. And his trophies were not only wives. Models, prostitutes, porn stars, beauty pageant contestants were fair game. If a Trump trophy tattoo -- a golden 'T'—where put on the thigh of each Trump conquest and they assembled in the Trump Tower lobby, the overflow would disrupt hotel operations for hours or days.

Guinness World Records should consider a new category for Trump: 'the only man on earth to purchase a beauty pageant so he could go into the ladies' dressing room backstage to ogle, preen and, if lucky, get a phone number or two.'

His friend, Jeffrey Epstein, fits the profile perfectly also. Both were on the prowl throughout their testosterone-peak years. Like his preference for fast food, Trump's sexual conquests were another appetite to satisfy at his whim. And the lucky ladies ought to be grateful they had a sampling of the private Donald. Oh! And a tattoo to memorialize it? Fabulous!

While misogynists have a peculiar disrespect for women, let us not forget this same arrogant disrespect meted out to a far greater portion of humanity. We estimate that only 16% of the world population is white and half of these are women. We can then estimate Trump is able to tolerate, and treat as near equals, less than 10% of humankind given his biases, bigotry, and racist claims. White male supremacists and avid members of the MAGA fan club are among the tiny cohort of people Trump has shown a modicum of affection rather than disdain.

If you are born a white female, your place on the Trump totem pole of disrespect is near the bottom. If you were a woman of color, you would be ignored completely unless subject to ridicule.

MALADROIT

maladroit adjective

Save Word

mal·adroit | \ ˌma-lə-ˈdrȯit \

Definition of *maladroit*

: lacking adroitness : INEPT

While Trump has carefully constructed a mythical reputation for shrewd business dealings promoted and perpetuated by public relations gimmicks, flattering books, and by "The Apprentice," there are also books and articles that debunk this myth.

With six corporate bankruptcies in his portfolio and a tenacious resistance to divulge his tax returns or financial records, one is correctly suspicious of his claims of business astuteness.

Other telltale signs are his promotion of ill-prepared staff such as a bodyguard to corporate officer. His bevy of lawyers include crackpots with unethical tendencies. He surrounds himself with inept advisors selected not for independent thinking but to deepen and abet whatever he pursues. 'Yes-men' only may apply. These are Mafia-like practices. How his executive image could rise to such heights is truly remarkable as it is preposterous.

Lastly, that his father had to rescue him financially is further proof that Trump tarnished the family legacy rather than enhance it, contrary to widespread belief.

His pitiful performance as president of the United States cements his personal legacy of failure. Already ranking among the least capable commanders in chief, historians will find it difficult to resist ranking him 'dead-last' with the passage of decades.

PHONY

phony adjective
Save Word
pho·ny | \ ˈfō-nē \
variants: *or less commonly* **phoney**
phonier; phoniest

Definition of *phony* (Entry 1 of 4)
: not genuine or real: such as
a (1) : intended to deceive or mislead
    (2) : intended to defraud : COUNTERFEIT

Trump has built such a façade that a tragically significant percent of the U.S. electorate adores him. I am reminded of Saturday morning wrestling on TV where celebrity wrestlers perform rather than compete. I am reminded of itinerant preachers who claim to heal and prop their pseudo-crippled cronies in the congregation to come forward for miraculous healing, walking again without crutches to the outcries of hallelujahs from stunned onlookers.

The most divisive of phoniness is the "Big Lie." It has sapped the integrity from our democratic norms and practices. Unable to accept and face defeat, Trump's restoration crusade now dominates state legislative agendas, inspires devious gerrymandering, and threatens all future electoral processes.

The Republican party is now 'hollow-ed out' from blind obedience. Its purpose is not to govern; its mission is self-preservation at any cost. Pathetic and phony indeed.

IMPERVIOUS

impervious adjective

Save Word

im·per·vi·ous | \ (,)im-'pər-vē-əs \

Definition of *impervious*

1   a   : not allowing entrance or passage : IMPENETRABLE
        // a coat *impervious* to rain

    b   : not capable of being damaged or harmed
        // a carpet *impervious* to rough treatment

2   : not capable of being affected or disturbed
    // *impervious* to criticism

Do not try lecture Trump, you are treading 'on thin ice.' Of course, he can lecture you; but no reciprocity. My generation will readily recall the *Johnny Carson Tonight Show*. One of his endearing comic characters was *Carnac the Magnificent*, the all-knowing soothsayer. Trump also fashions himself as enlightened and brilliant.

Even a greater transgression, do not criticize Trump, you have fallen through the ice. Causing a blow to his fragile Ego is near suicidal if you dare; the half-life of a Trump "yes-man" marked by a mistaken comment that Trump takes as a slight. Any insights or learnings that criticism might evoke rolls off Trump's back like rain off a duck. Perfection is impervious to improvements.

Sitting on the high throne of the U.S. presidency, Trump presumes to share a rare gift that very few proclaim including the Pope; that is, infallibility. He cannot error. So, he is indeed impervious to criticism or correction. Trump's infinite capacity for self-aggrandizement and arrogance boggles the mind of us mere mortals.

FABRICATOR

fabricate verb

Save Word

fab·ri·cate | \ˈfa-bri-ˌkāt\
fabricated; fabricating

Definition of *fabricate*

transitive verb

1   a   : INVENT, CREATE
       b   : to make up for the purpose of deception
            // accused of *fabricating* evidence

Had Trump the diligence and perseverance to earn a PhD like his smart and discerning niece, Mary Trump's PhD (*Psychology*), his major would be *Fabrication*, summa cum laude. His Twitter mouthpiece served up lie after lie ad nauseum. Fabrications were often not even his own invention, but recitations of favorite distortions he saw aired on Fox News, normally spewing them out within the same news cycle.

Most utterances from Trump's mouth begin on a premise of righteous deceit, not fact, unless that fact bolsters his position. The stuff of propaganda begins with promoting advantage, not truth. Truth is an inconvenience Trump eschews whenever necessary.

Of course, topping thousands of small or medium lies is the "Big Lie." Tragically, Trump supporters have weaned on a diet of lies for so long, they cannot differentiate truth from fiction. And evidence has no place in the matter. Our democracy may fall due to the corrosive use of fabrication as a political imperative.

OPSTREPEROUS

obstreperous adjective

🔖 Save Word

ob·strep·er·ous | \ əb-ˈstre-p(ə-)rəs 🔊, äb- \

Definition of *obstreperous*

1 : marked by <u>unruly</u> or aggressive noisiness : <u>CLAMOROUS</u>
// *obstreperous* merriment
// an *obstreperous* argument

2 : stubbornly resistant to control : <u>UNRULY</u>
// *obstreperous* behavior
// an *obstreperous* child

Obstreperous is another word for tantrum. A hallmark of a Trump rally is his childish, brutish rants. Like a mob boss accosting his underlings sitting at the kitchen table eating pasta, Trump erupts into a tirade that everyone must patiently endure in rapt attention, nodding and yelling in approval.

Trump delivers boisterous bombshell cliches and insults perfect for repetition echoing from his adoring crowds. Suggestive of "Heil Hitler," Trump knows how to stir a crowd into a frenzy. Just ask Hillary Clinton. "Lock her up!" was one such common refrain.

It typified Trump's ability to choreograph and arouse the animus of his faithful.

January 6th marks the apex of Trumpian rants as it incited rioting, massive storming the U.S. Capitol resulting mayhem, destruction, and death. Trump's obstreperous provocations is the 'red meat' he serves up to his devotees. And they relish this diet.

DOGMATIC

dogmatic adjective
Save Word
dog·mat·ic | \ dȯg- ma-tik 🔊, däg- \
variants: *or less commonly* **dogmatical** \ dȯg- ma-ti-kəl 🔊, däg- \

The "Big Lie" is now Republican political dogma. It is the spark that ignites voter restricting legislation, audits, court challenges, protests, gerrymandering, electoral mischief of all kinds.

Governing is no longer of the people, by the people and for the people. Special interests now rule through their Republican surrogates, and the "Big Lie" is the remedy for a growing diversity in the populace that threatens their status quo.

Derived from the Greek 'dogma' (δόγμα) meaning "that which one thinks is true," the word belongs on the Trump 'Coat of arms.' Like a broken hit record, his "Big Lie" remains at the top of the charts.

He has proven the adage that repetition breeds certainty. If he declared the earth is the center of our solar system, debunking Galileo, it will promptly become gospel in public school science curricula. Such is the blind observance to Trump lies.

And so, Dear Donald, why not espouse this as astronomic Big Lie #2? Let us also rename planet Jupiter after you. Planet Trump is perfect. It is about time you get celestial accolades.

HIPPOCRITICAL

hypocritical adjective

🔖 Save Word

hyp·o·crit·i·cal | \ ˌhi-pə-ˈkri-ti-kəl 🔊 \

Definition of *hypocritical*

: characterized by behavior that contradicts what one claims to believe or feel : characterized by hypocrisy

An unscrupulous liar has no trouble flip-flopping to suit their present circumstances. A particularly good example is Trump overinflating his books to leverage borrowing and underinflating his books to minimize taxes. He is intelligent enough – cunning is more accurate -- to know when saying or tweeting something he knows to be untrue is more advantageous. Such is his audacity that even though public evidence to contrary is mainstream, available, he proclaims the falsehood with the demeanor of a saintly piety.

A person like Trump is prone to hypocrisy at every turn. He lacks core integrity or principle. Father Fred made sure his moral compass was fixed on self-interest only, not on any universal human value or community good. Belief or inner conviction turned into unadorned pragmatism.

UNSCRUPULOUS

unscrupulous adjective

🔖 Save Word

un·scru·pu·lous | \ ˌən-ˈskrü-pyə-ləs 🔊 \

Definition of *unscrupulous*
: not scrupulous : UNPRINCIPLED

Add up all the deceit, conceit, exaggeration, profanity, infidelity – the list goes on and on – and you can bundle this assortment of unbecoming in one word: unscrupulous. Trump shares with a three-month-old baby, the psychopath, and the sociopath. No or little concept of right or wrong; no or little regard for the environment, family, or community; no or a faint conscious; no guard rails.

A rich man can get away with this; few others can. He weaponized the legal profession to insulate himself from consequences most others face. Atonement has never been a requirement in Trump's life. Redemption is for saps who cannot beat the system or the rap. If he manages to destroy American democracy, he will be a hero because his drained the swamp and Made America Great Again. Great for whom? Thugs and tyrants?

BORING

boring adjective

🔖 Save Word

bor·ing | \ ˈbȯr-iŋ 🔊 \

Definition of *boring*
: causing weariness and restlessness through lack of interest : causing boredom : TIRESOME
// a *boring* lecture

There can be nothing more boring than sitting with a self-absorbed, boastful misogynist spewing verbal bull and expecting rapt attention and affirmation after each profane utterance.

Trump requires this of his avid followers. In his presence, do not ever expect to be the center of attention; reserved only for 'the Donald.' Your thoughts and feelings have no place at his table; so, do not be so bold as to anticipate reciprocity. You are not so lucky or so entitled in his presence.

The oxygen in the room belongs to Trump. Stay awake though; falling asleep is a mortal sin. Do not show or admit boredom; that is a felony. Smile when Donald smiles; frown when Donald frowns; pout when Trump pouts. That is Trump etiquette. Better learn it and behave or you will not be allowed to return.

If you want an expensive boring weekend, book a room at Mar-a-Lago and shadow Trump wherever he appears in public. The main attraction is not the beach. When you make a pilgrimage to venerate Trump, you are there to acquire indulgences and bragging rights. The current price is a huge bite from your wallet and intense boredom. But Mecca and Vatican cannot compete.

BRAGGART

brag·gart
/ˈbragərt/ 🔊

noun

1. a person who boasts about achievements or possessions:
   "braggart men"

A confident and secure person lets others provide the accolades. Trump is not that person. They do not need to drum-up gratuitous applause. Trump is like a carnival barker when it comes to braggadocio. His rallies are self-indulgent lovefests dedicated to the proposition that Trump is all-knowing, all-wonderful, all-virtuous, all-discerning, all-mighty, all-truth, all-omnipotent.

Sap from maple trees cannot emit the nectar a Trump rally oozes. Crowd size is Trump's measuring device of self-worth second only to noise. Bragging rights is Trump's trophy case; he accumulates, invents, and displays his victories whenever and wherever a receptive person or crowd will listen, admire, and applaud his self-proclaimed preeminence.

JUANDICED

jaundiced adjective

Save Word

jaun·diced | \ jȯn-dəst, jän- \

Definition of *jaundiced*

1 : affected with or as if with jaundice

2 : exhibiting or influenced by envy, distaste, or hostility
   // a *jaundiced* eye

Anything that detracts from, contradicts, impedes, overtakes, challenges, competes with, or belittles anything Trumpian has just entered the domain deserving his jaundiced disdain. No matter if protected by free speech, any blog, news report, court finding, photo, expose, book, press release, comment, protest deserve vilification and rejection either from a Trump tweet, or comments by Kelly Ann Conway or other spokesperson. And if the irritation is huge enough, ready yourself for threat of a libel suit which might follow no matter if it has any merit. Be prepared to defend, and spend, yourself in court.

PAMPERED

pampered adjective

Save Word

pam·pered | \ ˈpam-pərd \

Definition of *pampered*

: treated with extreme or excessive care and attention

Mar-a-lago is his "nursery pen" where catering and adulation cover him like a soft blanket. The 'silver' spoon – sorry, the 'golden' spoon – is still in his mouth after 74 years of coddling, entitlement, luxury, doting, impulse, appetite religiously catered and satisfied.

We do not know if someone wipes his ass, but that time may come. Do not even think about a 3-ply tissue. Only imported Egyptian 1000 thread wash clothes -- disposable of course -- will do. A hand-picked nurse with a tiny waistline will do as well. Oh, the sexy outfit is necessary too.

One can only speculate what his hairdo looks like in the wee hours: likely, the prime rationale for sleeping alone. Melanie would get nightmares sleeping next to Trump absent his perfect coiffure that artfully spreads his locks like fog over a mountain top, pampered better than Tsar Nicholas II Romanov's family pet elephant.

FIXATED

fixated adjective

Save Word

fix·at·ed | \ fik-ˌsā-təd \

Definition of *fixated*
: arrested in development or adjustment
especially : arrested at a pregenital level of psychosexual development

While it may be malpractice to diagnose without a license, it is still permissible to render a suspicion that borders on psychiatric pronouncement. The arrested development and immaturity so remarkable in countless utterances, decisions and actions in plain sight make it abundantly clear to even a layperson that Trump fixated somewhere along the infantile, boyhood and pubescent stages. Of course, his duped followers are oblivious.

Confined to leading his family-owned dynasty wreaked enough havoc already. But to lead the most powerful country on earth with the maturity of a fourth grader has been a disaster. Surrounding himself with playmates rather than professionals, most without government expertise, has amplified the destructive consequences. Of course, the Republican congress used the period to prop up and cater to the interests of the wealthy and corporate lobbyists.

We must make special mention of the fixation that Trump displayed by his unexplainable deference to Vladimir Putin and Kim Jong-un. To declare that he and the Korean dictator exchanged love letters was absurd and had no discernible impact on relations anyway. Such pandering can be explained by his reverence for status and power, and a devotion for tyranny that is antithetical for a leader of a democracy.

DISLOYAL

disloyal adjective

Save Word

dis·loy·al | \ (ˌ)dis-ˈlȯi(-ə)l \

Definition of *disloyal*
: lacking in loyalty
also : showing an absence of allegiance, devotion, obligation, faith, or support
// his *disloyal* refusal to help his friend

Greyhound Lines does not have enough buses. As president, Trump threw so many former associates 'under the bus' Greyhound had to beg GM for more production. This is another idiomatic phrase that if not coined before, Trump would have inspired it.

What is as tragic and regrettable, not only people found themselves crushed under the bus; the U.S. Constitution, our allies, NATO, environmental regulations, trade agreements, minorities, women's rights, civil rights, science, medicine tossed under as well.

Not out of conviction, but his bravado and rank appeal to his base political class bent on rendering government impotent, snubbing world institutions, and serving the special interests of corporations and the wealthy.

IMPETUOUS

impetuous adjective

Save Word

im·pet·u·ous | \ im-ˈpech-wəs ; -ˈpe-chə-, -chü-əs \

Definition of *impetuous*
1 : marked by impulsive vehemence or passion
// an *impetuous* temperament

Faithful insiders, speaking off the record or after they leave their positions, often recount Trump's tendency for outbursts and lashing out. On demand satisfaction is his modus operandi including on policy matters. Impetuosity requires 'yes-men' and 'yes-women' or he will erupt like a tea pot over the slightest transgression or irritation.

Any unflattering news, inconvenience, unpleasant surprise, or advice suggesting he reconsider or change course could trigger a fit of anger, resentment, or castigation. So, most Trumpian mealymouthed cronies learned to stay out of his 'line of fire.' Like a home where domestic abuse is prevalent, the Oval Office was filled with eggshells -- and not just on Easter. Watch your step!

PATHETIC

pathetic adjective

Save Word

pa·thet·ic | \ pə-'the-tik \

Definition of *pathetic*

1 : having a capacity to move one to either compassionate or contemptuous pity

2 : marked by sorrow or melancholy : SAD

3 : pitifully inferior or inadequate
// the restaurant's *pathetic* service

4 : ABSURD, LAUGHABLE
// a *pathetic* costume

To sum up, the totality of Trump's personality traits that animate his attitudes, thinking, decisions, preferences, judgements, and appetites render him a pathetic figure on multiple measures despite what a sizable minority of Americans and corrupted Republican Party proclaims in his defense. History will prove them wrong. This kind of pathetic is not worthy of sympathy, only scorn.

AFTERWORD

Blessed with advantages in terms of means, freedom, status, and opportunity, on thinks of Franklin Roosevelt in comparison to

Trump. Another aristocrat blessed with privileges few enjoy; FDR used his enriched upbringing to become a consummate public servant who successfully led the nation through tumultuous years. Remarkably, his did so after overcoming the debilitation of polio. He summoned inner strength to persevere and devoted years serving the common good. His legacy puts him among a handful of outstanding presidents.

Given a personality profile discussed here, had Trump succumbed to polio, it is difficult to envision he would have done anything but sulk and live a life of bitterness and self-pity. He did, however, enjoy good health, and only achieved mediocrity at best in business and as U.S. president if we are charitable in our assessment.

Just like Roosevelt, the 21st century's dealt Trump one of cruelest challenge in the Covid-19 pandemic. Aside from a laudable vaccine procurement, he utterly and miserably failed to lead America through this scourge. Instead, his trivialization and politization rejecting basic public health advice led to unnecessary mortality and morbidity on an unforgivable scale. History will render him a pathetic president on this account alone.

Made in the USA
Monee, IL
10 July 2022